MANAGEMENT IMMEMORIAL
Learnings from Literature

I0510482

JAGANATHAN T

INDIA · SINGAPORE · MALAYSIA

Notion Press

Old No. 38, New No. 6
McNichols Road, Chetpet
Chennai - 600 031

First Published by Notion Press 2019
Copyright © Jaganathan T 2019
All Rights Reserved.

ISBN 978-1-68466-035-3

असतोमा सद्गमय ।
तमसोमा ज्योतिर् गमय ।
मृत्योर्मामृतं गमय ॥
ॐ शान्ति शान्ति शान्तिः ॥

Asatomā sadgamaya
Tamasomā jyotirgamaya
Mrityormā amritamgamaya
Oṁ śhānti śhānti śhāntiḥ

From ignorance, lead me to truth;

From darkness, lead me to light;

From death, lead me to immortality

May there be peace

This book is a sincere attempt to move forward in the 'growth path,' from 'ignorance' to 'knowledge,' from 'darkness' to 'bright future,' from all 'negative vibes' to 'positive thinking.'

लोकाःसमस्ताःसुखिनोभवंतु॥

"May all beings everywhere be happy and free. May the thoughts and actions of our own life, contribute in some way, to the happiness and freedom for all."

This book is dedicated to my mother
Loganayaki who has dedicated
her life for my well-being.

Contents

 Contents

SECTION C – Leadership Traits

Foreword
By Prof. L.S. Ganesh

"Management Immemorial," the title of this book, will rouse expectations among potential readers including practitioners, academicians, students, and trainers immersed in the field, and maybe even the general public having a passing interest in the subject. All of them would expect that this book should contain important parts of all the wisdom gained over many decades of the theories and practices of the various bodies of knowledge constituting management. These would be in the form of precious nuggets and gems concerning the philosophy, principles, perspectives and practices of management. Readers will not be disappointed on this count.

While the functional aspects, viz., human resources, finance, marketing, operations (products and services), organizational systems, and strategy, have dominated the notions and mental models of management among all concerned, the need to gain knowledge and understanding of the integrative aspects—those that bind together all these functional aspects into a seamless whole—has never been more than now. Ethics, values and principles are the foundations of wise, proper and sustainable managerial actions. They are also the strongest integrative forces that bind the functions of management in theory and practice across thought, word and deed. Those nuggets and gems

are to be found not just within the core of management literature, but sometimes in the deeper oceans of recalled or codified wisdom literature present across all cultures and societies in our world. It is here that India is revered as the primal seed from which various wisdom traditions sprouted elsewhere.

The strong interest in knowing, understanding and using wisdom rooted in Indian philosophy, ethics and values for living a productive, fulfilling life has continued over many years in the professional world. In recent years, this has coincided with the exponential growth of the world of digital knowledge and experiences. Consequently, the eternal value of Indian wisdom traditions can potentially reach every nook and corner of our world, and offer timeless benefits to all who immerse themselves in the boundless ocean they are. Keeping in mind this eventuality, the author has dived into important regions in the ocean, searched and picked wonderful precious nuggets and gems. He now presents them to all stakeholders in management thought and practice, so that they may also partake of the wonder, the pure truths, the depths and brilliance of all the insights offered by peerless thinkers and guides whose words and works are now immortal. These words and works form the eternal maps and signposts along life's journeys that managers undertake in their organizations as well as homes.

The selection and presentation of the contents in this book are marked by a touch of class coupled with a keen sense of impact and balance. These are very evident from the structuring of the Sections into Attitudes and Skills and then further into their components. The author has referred to philosophers and thinkers across the ages ranging from Kautilya to Kalam, and has also drawn upon the wisdom contained in two of the greatest texts pertaining to our lives, viz., the Gita and Thirukkural. The book is studded with quotes, examples, tabular summaries and visual presentations, all of which make it attractive and accessible.

This book deserves to be on the work tables of managers and executives, and actually no, not just there, but right in the core of the sub-consciousness of all decision-makers and problem-solvers.

L.S. Ganesh
Professor
Department of Management Studies
Indian Institute of Technology Madras
Chennai 600036.

Foreword
By H.R. Mohan

Having known Jagannathan for close to two decades as a techie with expertise in Enterprise Networking, Telecom and Contact Center Infrastructure, Information Security Consulting and Audit, I am amused to see his other side as an Author penning an inspirational and though provoking book *"MANAGEMENT IMMEMORIAL: Learnings from Literature"* providing valuable insights for self-development of an individual.

While there are a number of books available in this area of management, this book appears to be unique in compiling and presenting the pearls of wisdom from most popular and respectable ancient literature of India (Bhagavad Gita, Tirukkural), philosophers (Ramanujacharya, Kabirdas, Tulsidas), thinkers (Chankya, Tagore) and leaders (Subramanya Bharati, Kalam) known to us but taken for granted. Jagan's efforts in converting his random thoughts published as "Monday Musings" blog posts over a period time into a structured, handy and useful publication to highlight the importance of life skills and impart them is highly laudable.

Jagan, while claims to explain in this book, just five skills each under three chapters – Attitudes, Skills and Leadership Traits, actually touches and educates on almost all aspects of self-management, leadership and life skills through quotes, examples drawn from day to day life,

anecdotes & stories, reference tables, illustrations and visuals which makes an impact in learning and reinforces the understanding through the chapter-end takeaways. The presentation is easy to read and one can finish reading the entire book in one go.

The book starts with a section explaining "Attitudes" since it determines the individual's altitude. One's attitudes towards work, positive thinking, avoiding procrastination, perseverance and dreaming big have a major role in the individual's growth.

In the second section on skills, five fundamental skills – Learning, Listening, Process Excellence, Communication Skill and Team Work are discussed at length.

In the present context of VUCA (Volatile, Uncertain, Complex and Ambiguous) eco system threatening the enterprises, a quality leader makes a lot of difference in steering the enterprises to achieve excellence. The third and final section covers the leadership traits such as delegation, taking ownership, leading, confidence building and mentoring the subordinates.

I consider this book will be an asset for professionals who are already employed and aspiring to advance in their career as well as the students to learn the essential life skills for their future, faculty members and trainers to teach these skills to the needy.

H.R. Mohan

Editor, IEEE India Info, India Council Newsletter
Chairman, ACM India Chennai Chapter
Chair (2006–2015), IEEE Computer Society, Madras
President (2013–2014), Computer Society of India
Former Associate Vice President (Systems), The Hindu.

Acknowledgments

I start the book in exactly the style you will find in the rest of this book. I start with a *Thirukkural*[1].

நன்றி மறப்பது நன்றன்று நன்றல்லது
அன்றே மறப்பது நன்று.

The meaning of this *kural* goes like this, "It is not good to forget forever a help received but better to forget a bad deed then and there."

My first acknowledgment is due to the innumerable management gurus Thiruvalluvar, Bharathiyar, Tagore, Vyasa and many more, who gave us these management mantras, which are to be preserved and cherished.

Special thanks to Prof. L.S. Ganesh, Department of Management Studies, IITM, Chennai for writing a valuable foreword. I have interacted with him for the past five years and have gained immensely from his knowledge, humility and gentleness.

Special thanks to Mr. HR Mohan for writing a very valuable foreword for the book. Mohan is a good industry friend.

---

[1]Thirukkural is a classical literature of 1,330 short and meaningful poems of seven words each, written by Thiruvalluvar.

Special thanks to my wife, Bhooma VG, who has always been a source of learning for me. She has been a well-wisher in the form of a critic (constructive criticism). I was emboldened to bring out this book as the blogs received her acceptance and appreciation. I go to her every time I get a compelling idea and need to structure it into a framework. She did the same for this book. I went to her when I wanted a captivating title and cover design for this book!

Thanks to my staff, friends and my Social Media readers who have appreciated me and encouraged me to continue writing this. Special thanks to Jay Shankar, a LinkedIn friend, who read and commented on all the 25 episodes of *Monday Musings* and shared many useful tips and videos for use. I used them to improve the content of this book. Such is the power of Social Media.

Thanks to Prasad PK from AGS Health (India) Private Limited who had contributed with a few interesting quotes some of which have been used in this book.

My father-in-law, Govindarajan VR, is a personification of the idea that age is only a number. He is starting a research book at the age of 84. Thanks to him for sharing a few valuable inputs for this book. More than the inputs, thanks for the enthusiasm and the encouragement. Enthusiasm spreads.

Acknowledgments for my many mentors who have left a strong influence in me. I have acknowledged the efforts of a few of them in this book. There are several more who have helped me reach where I have and do what I have done.

Special thanks to my colleagues, Sandhya and Manikandan, who have helped with editing and compiling this book.

Thanks to *Samskrita Bharati* (an organization doing yeomen service to spread Sanskrit as a spoken language) which has aroused the curiosity in me to learn the beautiful language Sanskrit.

Thanks to Notion Press team without their support I could not have brought out this book.

My sincere gratitude to 'CIO Association' (CiO Klub) for volunteering to release the book in their banner.

Thanks in advance for the readers who can give feedback and suggestions. I learnt to practice gratitude for peace and happiness including expressing gratitude in anticipation. Thiruvalluvar has covered every aspect of Leadership in his Thirukkural including the value of feedback and constructive criticism. I cannot help but jump the gun and start with that concept here itself.

இடிக்குந் துணையாரை யாள்வரை யாரே
கெடுக்குந் தகைமை யவர். *(447)*

Translation of the Above Kural: Those who develop the habit of listening to feedback including constructive criticism, and those who develop companions who can give constructive criticism, can never be defeated. The goal in constructive criticism is to critique an individual so

they will benefit or improve to achieve success. A good professional should take criticism on board and not respond as though it is a personal attack and should instead make it work to their advantage.

I want to follow these ideals of Thiruvalluvar and would therefore cherish feedback including 'constructive criticism.' This is my first attempt as an author and your feedback matters a lot to me. Share your feedback by sending email to tjaganthan22@gmail.com

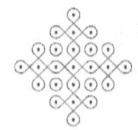

Preface

MONDAY MUSINGS
– The seeds that grew into this book

The inspiration for this book came from two unconnected and incidental events that happened on the same day about a year back.

I was invited as an honorary Board of Studies member to *VelTech School of Management* in Chennai. It was a meeting organized to finalize the curriculum for their management courses. While perusing through their curriculum, I noticed a mention about the topic *Thirukkural[1] and Management* as a subject for internal Project Work. I used to think that Thirukkural is a classical treatise on *Dharma and life*, but this incident aroused my interest to look at it from a different perspective.

It was a Friday.

On the same evening, one of my peers in a meeting was ecstatic, saying, "Thank God, It's Friday." I asked him if he was really so relieved to be away from work. And consequently, If he was aware of the expression *Yogaha*

---

[1] *Thirukkural is a classical literature of 1,330 short and meaningful poems of seven words each, written by Thiruvalluvar.*

karmasu kausalam as explained in *Bhagavad Gita²*, to which he answered negatively.

The two incidents above kindled my thoughts on the need for positive work attitudes based on 'Indian classical works.' I researched on similar efforts. I could see a lot of material on the Internet on isolated works such as 'Thirukkural and Management' and 'Bhagavad Gita and Management.' But, a comprehensive study of management education using Literature, were not many to find. I decided to take up the mantle and take the first step in this direction.

India has contributed a lot of popular and good concepts to this world such as yoga, meditation, ayurveda, bharatanatyam, etc. I find Indian literature another great contribution to the globe. After all, India has given to this world the concept of 'Vasudaiva kutumbakam' (in Sanskrit from Upanishad) and 'Yadhum Ore Yavarum Kelir' (in Tamil by *Kanian Poongundranar*). Both mean the same, i.e.,'the entire world is just one family.' 'I created a weekly communication, initially in the form of an email to all my staff and close contacts, sent every Monday as a motivation message so as to start the work week on a positive note.' Encouraged by the positive response, I extended the same as a weekly blog on LinkedIn and Twitter under the topic 'Monday Musings.'

Monday Musings came promptly before 9 a.m. every Monday, consistently for 25 weeks.

'MONDAY MUSINGS' blogs received interest and positive feedback from many of my staff and my social network contacts.

---

² *Bhagavad Gita is the dharmic discourse in Mahabharatham given by Lord Krishna to Arjuna during the Kurukshetra war.*

Encouraged by the interest and feedback from the readers of the blog messages, I decided to convert this into a book and thus this book emerged.

Why Management through Literature? I find quotes are powerful tools for communicating a message. The impact and reach of quotes are at once, strong and widespread. Similarly, a concept when learnt through beautiful poems goes deeper and stays longer. Please try it yourself.

Why a new book when there is research information available on this subject? This is not research material. My intention is to explain certain 'life skills,' using the references in Indian Literature and my personal experience. This book would be a new dimension in understanding management.

I have liberally used quotes from Tamil and Sanskrit, two classical Indian Languages. There used to be a few complaints as to why I ignored other Indian Languages which are also rich in Literature. Unfortunately, I know only Tamil, Sanskrit and Hindi among 50+ Indian Languages. There are many more interesting quotes from other Indian Languages as well. I would be happy to learn and include other Indian Languages in my further works.

Motivational Mondays

Many of you would have heard of the famous or infamous expression TGIF, i.e., *Thank God It's Friday* (or Thank Goodness it's Friday). The idea is to create commercial euphoria about weekend entertainment. There are restaurants, bars, even TV programs on TGIF.

The unintended upshot is of course *Oh God, It's Monday.* I have heard many people cribbing *Oh God, It's Monday.* When I ask for a meeting, generally people don't prefer Mondays. When there is a choice, it always gets pushed to Tuesdays or Wednesdays. Mondays aren't usually the favorite day of the week.

What Is the Ideal Day and Time for Meetings?

[1]According to a study from YouCanBookMe, a UK company, 2:30 p.m. Tuesdays are the best days for weekly meetings. This is arrived at based on two million responses to 530,000 invitations. What is the rationale behind this? 2:30 p.m. Tuesday is the time most people are free and accept the meetings, and hence attendance is highest. The most likely days for people to be out of the office are Mondays and Fridays. It was found out that only one in three people accept meeting invites on Mondays.

But what if you want to set a meeting time to optimize performance and not just attendance? Research into fatigue and behavior suggests that the time of day makes a difference in how we process information. As the week progresses and the day wears on, we tire, and that affects our decisions.

[2]Jonathan Levav, from Columbia University and his colleagues looked at more than 1,000 rulings made in 2009 by eight judges. They found that the likelihood of a favorable ruling peaked at the

---

[1] *Reference taken from* https://qz.com/work/653033/
heres-the-best-day-and-time-to-hold-a-meeting/

[2] *Reference taken from https://www.theguardian.com/law/2011/apr/11/
judges-lenient-break*

beginning of the day, steadily declining over time from a probability of about 65% to nearly zero, before spiking back up to about 65% after a break for a meal or snack. They were clearly subjected to a phenomenon called 'Decision Fatigue.' **Decision Fatigue** is applicable for everyone and not only these judges. What is Decision Fatigue?

> Decision Fatigue is the deteriorating quality of decisions made by an individual after a long session of Decision Making.

In my experience, the best time for a weekly meeting is Monday mornings. In my company, we schedule our weekly review meeting on Monday mornings, probably a little later in the morning, say around 11 a.m. to get enough time for preparations. I find energy levels high and better participation during this time.

Magnificence of Musings

Musings form part of a powerful and pertinent title in this series. Musings as per Cambridge Dictionary means, "*thoughts* or *comments* on something you have been *thinking about carefully* and for a *long time*."

There is a significant difference between எண்ணம் (ennam), which is the translation of thought, and சிந்தனை (chinthanai), which is the translation of musing.

Thoughts are not synonymous with musings Musing is much more powerful than thought. Musings are focused and considered thoughts, developed over a period of time. We need to practice to 'muse' quite often. I have heard people saying that they get powerful ideas while musing

alone, sitting in a quiet ambience. I make it a practice to 'muse' for a few minutes on a daily basis. This is a useful and powerful practice for our mind. So much so that our *Vedas* proclaim that the Supreme Lord created the Universe as an outcome of his musings.

Thoughts will only come to the person who has the ability to achieve the same. If you are getting any thought, don't ignore it. Muse and work on your thought seriously because thoughts select people. You have the potential to achieve and that is why the thought has chosen you. Thought itself has the power of attracting the resources to fulfill the process.

"You are today where your thoughts have brought you. You will be tomorrow where your thoughts take you."

— James Allen

This book has been structured into three sections viz. Aspirational Attitudes, Springboarding Skills and Leadership Traits.

What is the difference between Attitudes and Skills?

Skills are acquired through practice than education. Attitudes are practiced through transformation. Transformational change is required to perfect positive attitudes.

Leaders of course need to practice the attitudes and learn the skills given in the first two sections. And then, leaders need to continue further by developing certain additional traits. These traits are covered in the last section.

All chapters in this book are 'essential life concepts' practiced and perfected by our forefathers as could be seen in our literature. This common thread, 'learning from the literature' binds the ideas presented in the book. – i.e— literature to leadership. Each chapter has 'Take Aways' at the end for a quick recap too.

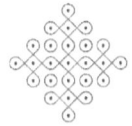

Classical to Contemporary – Thought Leaders Referred To in This Book

An introduction to the thinkers whose thoughts form the core of this book, is listed here in chronological sequence – classical to contemporary.

Bhagavad Gita

The Bhagavad Gita meaning *The Song of God,* often referred to as the Gita, is a scripture in Sanskrit that is a part of the Hindu epic *Mahabharata.* Gita is elucidated primarily as a dialogue between Lord Krishna and his friend and cousin, Arjuna. The Gita consists of 700 slokas in 18 chapters.

At the start of the *Dharma Yudhha* (righteous war) between the Pandavas and Kauravas at Kurukshetra, Arjuna, a Pandava prince, faces a moral dilemma and despairs about the violence and death the war will cause. He wonders if he should renounce and seeks Krishna's counsel, whose answers and discourse constitute the Bhagavad Gita. The Krishna-Arjuna dialogue covers a broad range of spiritual topics, touching upon ethical and philosophical issues that go far beyond the war.

Figure 1: Lord Krishna Mentoring Arjuna in Bhagavad Gita

The Gita is essentially the motivational speech by the world's greatest mentor, Sri Krishna to remove fear and instill confidence in the confused mind of his mentee, i.e., Arjuna. Gita is liberally used in this book to explain various management concepts.

Kautilya – Chanakya

Figure 2: Kautilya Aka Chanakya

Kautilya, also known as *Chanakya,* was believed to be the chief minister in the court of *Chandragupta Maurya,* a contemporary of *Alexander* and the first great emperor of India who ruled the subcontinent in the 4th century BC. He is considered the author of *Arthashastra,* meaning texts on wealth. There are different versions of the period and the author of Arthashastra. The predominant view is that Arthashastra is written by Kautilya during 4th century BCE. Kautilya was the advisor and confidante who helped Chandragupta Maurya capture the empire from the Nandas.

Arthashastra includes about 6000 hymns and is a comprehensive manual on how a state ought to be ruled and administrated by a King and his administrators. It is very detailed and systematic in prescribing solutions to various problems associated with a monarchial form of governance. Several of the administrative suggestions prescribed by the author are still relevant and practicable in the modern administrative world.

Arthashastra is a precursor to the modern-day Process Manual/Quality Manual of an enterprise.

Thiruvalluvar

Figure 3: Thiruvalluvar

Thiruvalluvar, also known as *theivapulavar* (*a poet with divine capabilities*), was a celebrated Tamil poet and philosopher. He is best known for authoring *Thirukkuṛaḷ*, a classical collection of couplets.

Thirukkural is well structured, 1330 couplets divided into 133 chapters called 'Adhikarams,' with ten kurals in each Adhikaram. The entire work is divided into three sections titled, *Aram, Porul* and *Inbam* dealing with Dharma, Wealth and Love respectively. The structure is as follows:

- 38 Adhikarams (380 kurals) in Aram section.

- 70 Adhikarams (700 kurals) in Porul section.

- 25 Adhikarams (250 kurals) in Inbam section.

Each Kural consists of seven words, four in the first line and three in the second line. Thiruvalluvar had followed this pattern without deviation. Thirukkural adheres to *Venba* form of Tamil grammar called *yappilakanam*.

Purushartha (पुरुषार्थ) is a key concept in Hinduism and is used in many Hindu classical literatures. Purushartha is a composite Sanskrit word from *purusha* (पुरुष) and *artha* (अर्थ). Purusha means 'human being'; Artha means 'purpose.' Together, purushartha means 'purpose of a human being' or 'object of human pursuit.'

The four purusharthas as per the *Upanishads* are *Dharma* (righteousness and moral values), *Artha* (prosperity and economic values), *Kama* (pleasure, love and psychological values) and *Moksha* (liberation and spiritual values). Thirukkural focuses on the first three of the purusharthas (Dharma, artha, and kama) without delving into the fourth, i.e., moksha, suggesting that the proper pursuit of three will inevitably lead to the fourth.

The uniqueness of Thirukkural is in explaining great philosophies in just seven words. Thiruvalluvar has covered almost every topic one can think of. The text is considered as one of the finest works in Tamil literature.

There are differing opinions about Thiruvalluvar's period. It is not clear if Kautilya precedes Thiruvalluvar or otherwise. It is believed that he lived around the 2nd century BC.

Thirukkural has already been translated to almost all Indian Languages and many foreign languages.

Thirukkural is the most commonly used literature in this book.

Ramanujacharya

Figure 4: Acharya Ramanujacharya

Guru Ramanujacharya was a Hindu theologian, philosopher, and one of the most important exponents of *Sri Vaishnavism* tradition within Hinduism. He was a social reformer too. He is considered as one of the three Hindu theological proponents Ramanujar did not just preach but practically lived many Leadership Qualities in propagating Bhakti or devotion.

Ramanujacharya's 1000th birth anniversary was celebrated recently, i.e., in 2017. He was believed to have lived 120 years, i.e., from 1017 to 1137. He is believed to be the reincarnation of *Adhisesha,* who serves Lord Vishnu by offering himself as the Lord's bed.

Saint Kabirdas

Figure 5: Saint Kabirdas

Kabir was a 15th-century Indian mystic, poet and saint, whose *dohas* influenced the Bhakti movement. Kabir's verses are followed by Muslim sects, Hindus and are even found in Sikhism's scripture, *Guru Granth Sahib*. He was strongly influenced by his teacher, the Hindu bhakti leader, Ramananda.

Kabir's poems are in vernacular Hindi, borrowing from various dialects including *Awadhi* and *Braj*. They cover various aspects of life and call for a loving devotion for God. Kabir composed his verses with simple Hindi words. Most of his work is concerned with devotion, mysticism and discipline.

Rabindranath Tagore translated Kabir's poems into English known as *One Hundred Poems of Kabir.*

Saint Tulsidas

Tulsidas, also known as Goswami Tulsidas, was a Hindu saint and poet renowned for his devotion to Lord Shri Rama. Tulsidas wrote several popular works in Sanskrit and Awadhi.

Figure 6: Saint Tulsidas

He is best known as the author of the epic *Ramcharitmanas,* a rendering of the epic, Ramayana, in Awadhi, a vernacular dialect of Hindi.

There is a difference of opinion among biographers regarding the year of birth of Tulsidas, the popular one being the period 1532–1623.

Tulsidas was a prolific writer and has composed several works. Modern scholars attest that he wrote at least six major works and six minor works, the best known of which is the Ramcharitmanas. The other works include *RamlalaNahachhu, BarvaiRamayan, Parvati Mangal, Dohavali, Vairagya Sandipani* and *Vinaya Patrika.* The devotional hymn, *Hanuman Chalisa* is also attributed to him.

Subramanya Bharati

Figure 7: Subramanya Bharati

Bharathiyar is a much adored Tamil poet.

Chinnaswami Subramanya Bharati, also known as Bharathiyar, was a writer, poet, journalist, Indian independence activist and a social reformer from Tamil Nadu. Popularly known as Mahakavi Bharati, he was a pioneer of modern Tamil poetry and is considered one of the greatest Tamil literary figure.

He lived a very short life, only 39 years, between 1882 and 1921.

Like Thiruvalluvar, Bharathiyar wrote poems on varied subjects, including a few on management. His noteworthy contributions include poems on the Indian independence movement, women's liberation, social justice, devotional songs, etc.

Bharati's works have been translated into every major Indian language as well as several European languages, including English, French, German, Russian, and Czech.

Gurudev Rabindranath Tagore

Figure 8: Gurudev Rabindranath Tagore

Rabindranath Tagore was a Bengali poet. Mahatma Gandhi gave him the title 'Gurudev.'

Rabindranath Tagore was the first non-European to win the Nobel Prize for Literature in 1913. He has the rare distinction of having penned the national anthems for two nations. Yes. His compositions were chosen by two nations as national anthems: India's *Jana Gana Mana* and Bangladesh's *Amar Shonar Bangla*. Not only that. Even the composer of Sri Lanka's national anthem, *Ananda Samarakoon,* was a student of Tagore, and it is said the song is inspired by Tagore's style.

Tagore has excelled in many of the fine arts. He wrote novels, essays, short stories, travelogues, dramas, and thousands of songs. He composed 2,230 songs, created a whole new genre of music called Rabindra Sangeet and was a prolific painter.

Among his fifty-odd volumes of poetry are *Manasi* (The Ideal One), *Sonar Tari* (The Golden Boat), *Gitanjali* (Song Offerings), *Gitimalya* (Wreath of Songs), and *Balaka* (The Flight of Cranes). The English renditions of his poetry include *The Gardener, Fruit-Gathering,* and *The Fugitive.* Tagore's major plays are *Raja* (The King of the Dark Chamber), *Dakghar* (The Post Office), *Achalayatan* (The Immovable), *Muktadhara* (The Waterfall), and *Raktakaravi* (Red Oleanders). He is the author of several volumes of short stories and a number of novels, among them *Gora, Ghare-Baire* (The Home and the World), and *Yogayog* (Crosscurrents). Besides these, he wrote musical dramas, dance dramas, essays of all types, travel diaries, and two autobiographies, one in his middle years and the other shortly before his death in 1941. Tagore also left numerous drawings and paintings. Tagore was also a *Vaggeyakara* like Bharathiyar ie he composed music himself for some of his songs.

Dr. APJ Abdul Kalam

Figure 9: APJ Abdul Kalam

Avul Pakir Jainulabdeen Abdul Kalam, or APJ Abdul Kalam was an Indian scientist and educationist who played a leading role in the development of India's missile and nuclear weapons programs. He was the 11th President of India from 2002 to 2007. He remained committed to using science and technology to transform India into a developed country.

Kalam wrote several books, including an autobiography, *Wings of Fire*, and his vision for India, *India 2020*. Among his numerous awards were two of the country's highest honors, the Padma Vibhushan and the Bharat Ratna.

Kalam was a popular President, known fondly as 'People's President.' Kalam died in 2015 while delivering a lecture to the students at Shillong. His death elicited spontaneous grief from many citizens—the first non-politician to earn this honor.

His quotes have been liberally used in this book, including two interesting incidents from his biography.

Entharo Mahanubhavulu Anthariki Vandanam is a Telugu song meaning, "We have many great noble people, I bow my head in respect for all of them."

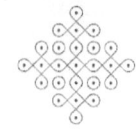

SECTION A

Five Aspirational Attitudes

"Your attitude, not your aptitude, will determine your altitude."

– Zig Ziglar

"Attitudes are nothing more than habits of thought."

– John C. Maxwell

पञ्च मनोभावा:

ஐந்து மனப்பான்மைகள்

Attitude Determines Altitude

"Your attitude, not your aptitude, will determine your altitude."

– Zig Ziglar

Attitudes have greater impact on life than aptitude. Hence, I put the section on 'Attitudes' ahead of 'Skills.'

Dr. Seligman's Study

[1]Dr. Seligman, author of the book 'Learned Optimism,' noticed an interesting fact from a long-term study of 1,500 people. Out of them, 83% of the people took their job because they believed they could make lots of money and the rest 17% took their job because they loved their job. Twenty years later, the two groups together had produced 101 millionaires. The amazing outcome is that only one of those millionaires came from the first group, but 100 of them came from the second group.

Even more amazing, is that, over 70% of those millionaires never went to college. And over 70% of those who became CEOs graduated in the bottom half of their class. Seligman concluded that it was their attitude, more than their aptitude that determined their altitude.

---

[1] Reference from https://www.drzimmerman.com/
tuesdaytip/5-take-it-to-the-bank-benefits-of-a-positive-attitude

What Indian Literature Says About Attitude

The central theme of this book is 'Personal Development' from Indian literature. I went about collecting references from Indian literature. Surprisingly, my observation was also very similar to that of Dr. Seligman's. I categorized the references collected by me under three broad categories, i.e., Attitudes, Skills and Leadership Traits. I found that most of the references went under the category Attitudes. That proved the adage, "Your attitude, not your aptitude, will determine your altitude." I decided to start the discussion with 'five amazing attitudes' for growth.

Let me start with a typical reference from Thirukkural. When I looked closely at this kural, I tend to think that Zig Ziglar would have got the motivation for his quote from this kural! (Remember, Thirukkural was written 2000 years back).

வெள்ளத் தனைய மலர்நீட்டம் மாந்தர்தம்
உள்ளத் தனையது உயர்வு. *(595)*

Transliteration (Tamil to English):

Vellaththanaiya malarnheettam maandhar dham
ullath thanaiyadhu uyarvu

Meaning – An aquatic flower raises its stem when the water level rises. Similarly, the height of achievement is dependent on the attitude of an individual.

I chose five of the attitudes which would be of immediate relevance to work and life. Of course, I smartly added a few more by clubbing similar ones under a single heading. Five attitudes taken here are:

1. **Work is Worship**

2. **Power of Positive Thinking**

3. **Avoiding Procrastination**

4. **Perseverance/Determination**

5. **Thinking Big/Dreaming Big**

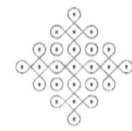

1. Work Is Workship

I am taking the help of the following literature references to illustrate the attitude 'Work is Worship.'

Table 1: Literature Reference for 'Work Is Worship'

Sl.	Illustration	Work	Reference	Author	Language	Remarks
1.	Uzhavukkum thozhilukum vandanai seivom	Bharathyiar Songs		Bharathiyar	Tamil	

There is nothing wrong in looking forward to an interesting weekend. But, 'Thank God It is Friday' gives a negative connotation that work is not enjoyable. Indian ethos stresses the theme 'Work is Worship.'

செய்யும் தொழிலே தெய்வம் –
அந்தத் திறமைதான் நமது செல்வம்

These are lyrics from a very popular Tamil song. This means 'Our work is God. Our Skill is Wealth.' This aptly describes our attitude towards work.

உழவுக்கும் தொழிலுக்கும் வந்தனை செய்வோம் – வீணில்
உண்டு களித்திருப்போரை நிந்தனை செய்வோம்

– The Great Tamil Poet Bharathiyar

Meaning – Let us respect agriculture and labor and criticize those who waste their precious time in eating and recreation.

Indian culture stands for 'respecting profession.' Indian literature equates work to God. As per Indian practice, one day of the famous nine-day *Navaratri* festival, i.e., *Ayudha Pooja,* is a celebration of 'profession.'

We should ideally make it **WHIM–W**ow! **H**appy **I**t is **M**onday!

I am neither an idealist nor a tyrant. I am not suggesting seven days of work nor am I saying that breaks or holidays are not important. I understand that taking a break is important for holistic life. I too have passions beyond my profession. I enjoy my holidays and I enjoy taking break with the family.

Let us flip it around. Rather than spending a week with expectations for the weekend, can we look forward to weekends as the time to ponder and recharge ourselves for the upcoming work week?

I look forward to Mondays. I look forward to the day when I would resume work.

I also sometimes hear advice from people asking us not to work too hard as it may not be good for health. Human physiology is designed for hard work. One does not get tired because of work. People get tired of doing 'uninteresting work' or 'stressful work.' People suffer due to stressful work and not because of 'overwork.'

Look forward to Mondays. It is the day to get back to your passion.

There is a common clamor to look for holidays. I have read reports that Dr. Abdul Kalam did not want the government to declare a holiday on his death.

Work and worship are necessary to take away the veil, to lift off the bondage and illusion.

— Swami Vivekananda

Love your work and make your work your passion. You can automatically remove the 'stress' from work. Make your work interesting and you will never feel tired.

How to identify your passion? It is that which does not make you tired. Vedas say that doing your passion creates the energy to sustain the work. Loving your work leads to taking pride in your work. It does not matter what work you do. Take pride in your work.

I quite often notice people making salutations to their work desk before starting their work.

But this experience is one of the reasons for me to include 'Work is Worship' as the first attitude.

I booked a cab to pick me up from Bengaluru City railway station by 5 a.m. in the morning. The driver was there promptly. Looking at him clean with the traditional religious marks of 'vibuthi and kumkum' on his forehead early in the morning was refreshing for me. I appreciated him and asked him if he had already bathed. The driver's answer stumped me. He replied, "This car is my livelihood. How can I touch my livelihood without taking a bath? I take a bath before starting my duty even if I have to start my duty by 2 a.m. in the morning."

Inspiring Story of Passionate 'Billionaire Barber'

Do you know the story of billionaire barber, Ramesh Babu, who drives around in his Rolls Royce Ghost? Ramesh Babu still prefers to cut hair so that he never forgets his humble beginnings.

He was only seven years old when his father, P. Gopal, a barber in Bengaluru, died. All he left behind was a barber shop. His mother had to work as a cook to help feed her children renting her husband's barber shop for Rs. 5 per day. He decided to run his father's salon after completing Higher Secondary education from St. Joseph's College of Commerce in Bengaluru. Babu bought a Maruti Omni people carrier for his personal use with the earnings from his salon. Then someone gave him the tip to rent the vehicle to 'Intel' that changed his life.

His Ramesh Tours and Travels is a flourishing business now. But he enjoys his work at his salon, Inner Space. "That's my bread and butter," he says about Inner Space.

An early riser, he checks his fleet before reaching the salon at eight in the morning. "Whatever I have achieved, there's nothing like giving a good haircut," he says.

Babu owes his success to doing what he thought was best. "Whatever I did, I did well, that's all I can say."

Take Aways

1. Do your work passionately. Passion will give the energy to do the work and take stress out of the work.

2. Give your best in whatever you do.

3. Respect your work. Worship your work. It is your livelihood.

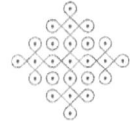

2. Power of Positive Thinking

Table 2: Literature Reference for 'Power of Positive Thinking'

Sl.	Illustration	Work	Reference	Author	Language	Remarks
1.	hatovaprāpsya-siswargaṁ	Bhagavad Gita	Chapter 2.37	Veda-vyasa	Sanskrit	Lord Krishna's advice to Arjuna
2.	Ennithuniga-karumam	Thirukkural	467, Chapter – 'Acting after due consideration'	Thiruvalluvar	Tamil	

What is **Positive Thinking**? Positive thinking is an attitude in which you always think about good and favorable results. A positive mind looks for happiness, health and a happy outcome to any situation. One who faces life with a positive attitude will always be more successful in life professionally as well as personally. A person with positive thinking anticipates happiness, health and success, and believes that he or she can overcome any obstacle and difficulty.

This is not just a management tool. There is science behind this. When you think and talk about what you want and how to get it, you feel happier and in greater control of your life. When you think about something that makes you happy, your brain *releases endorphins,* which give you a generalized feeling of well-being. Negative thoughts, words and attitude, create negative and unhappy feelings, moods and behavior. When the mind is negative, poisons are released into the blood, which causes more unhappiness and negativity. This is the way to failure, frustration and disappointment.

Both Positive Thinking and Negative Thinking are highly infectious. Be in the company of 'Positive Thinkers' to augment the power of Positive Thinking. That is how positive leaders create 'Positive and Engaged Teams.'

Positive Thinkers look for the good in every problem or difficulty. Even when things go wrong, they find positive outcomes from the situation.

I will take the help of Bhagavad Gita to explain this. Yes, Gita has a beautiful *sloka* on Positive Thinking. Surprised? Gita quotes many other management concepts as well.

हतो वा प्राप्स्यसि स्वर्गं जित्वा वा भोक्ष्यसे महीम् ।
तस्मादुत्तिष्ठकौन्तेययुद्धायकृतनिश्चयः ॥ 2.37॥

Hato vā prāpsyasi swargaṁ jitvāvā bhokṣhyase mahīm
tasmād uttiṣhṭha kaunteya yuddhāya kṛita-niśhchayaḥ

The literal translation of this sloka is:

If you fight, you will either be slain on the battlefield and go to the celestial abodes, or you will gain victory and enjoy the kingdom on earth. Therefore, arise with determination, O son of Kunti, and be prepared to fight.

The untold meaning is as follows:

Don't hesitate to go forward in the right path thinking about possible failure. Krishna makes it very simple. Arjuna's duty is to fight. Don't start a fight fearing about a possible failure in the war. It will be easy to win the battle if you engage in the battle with the confidence that you will win the battle.

Make every action a *Win-Win* strategy. Don't start a job thinking about the losses. Many times, losses have to be taken as investments for future gains. Would it not be an excellent idea to think, 'I achieve intended benefits if I win and I gain precious knowledge and experience if I lose.' This is what Krishna preached in the Gita.

Whenever we try for complex projects, I hear rejoinders from my colleagues such as, "It is difficult to win this opportunity as we have to fight against much bigger and stronger competitors." My response generally would be, "Does it matter? Give a good fight. We get the contract if we win and gain good knowledge on how to succeed the next time if we lose. Nothing to lose either way."

Positive Thinking should not be misunderstood as the irrational behavior of not assessing the risk of failure. A Positive Thinker is not afraid of the result. He/She counts failures as stepping stones for success.

What Are the Characteristics of a Positive Thinker?

A Positive Thinker is an optimist who looks for opportunities in every problem, who readily thinks of solution(s) for every problem and is someone who never looks back except for learning. A Positive Thinker thinks that everything that happens has something which can have good outcome.

I constantly hear people cribbing, "It is my misfortune that I always land in tough situations. I always have to resolve tough problems, etc."

I tell my colleagues, "Challenges are opportunities given by God to prove our mettle. Anyone can handle normal situations; only champions can handle a challenging situation. If you want to become a champion, enjoy challenges."

I have experienced this on many occasions in my career. One of the toughest challenges in a customer's project led to a series of system failures to the point of giving up. It made me spend a few sleepless nights at the project site. But on successfully completing the task, my position became more prominent in my company, and the industry. I have seen customers developing a close relationship with us and giving more orders because of hard and sincere efforts put in to resolve a difficult problem. There were enough instances of tough challenges turning into big opportunities. Take up the challenges hoping for possible opportunities from the challenges rather than the difficulties associated with them. That will give the energy to face the tough challenge.

Positive thinking recognizes that no problem is too large and that every problem has a solution if you are determined to look for it. It's important to cultivate positive thinking as a skill.

> **Idea** – Start an exclusive corner for 'Positive Messages' in your work place as well as home. Try this simple technique and the benefits would be enormous.

Figure 10: Good Message Board

Is *'Positive Thinking'* the same as *'Optimism'*?

Yes, in many ways, but there is a finer difference. Optimistic thinking tends to focus on the idea that everything will work out. It is possible that an Optimist can at times be blindsided by situations that occur and not be prepared for them. Positive thinking, on the other hand, acknowledges that problems can occur and that everything won't automatically work out unless one is prepared for it. Positive thinking embraces possibilities and looks for solutions without the assumption that everything will automatically work.

A 'Positive Thinker' thinks that everything is possible but does not necessarily think that everything needs to be executed. A Positive Thinker assesses every situation before taking up a task.

Thiruvalluvar has explained this well in multiple couplets.

The general explanation of this kural is: **Any task should be taken up only after detailed planning.**

Thinking about a plan after the task is taken up is wrong.

I would interpret this little differently. The Tamil word 'Enni' translates to 'assessment' more aptly than 'planning.' This 'kural' is a sample for 'Decision Making' (and not regretting a decision taken).

எண்ணித் துணிக கருமம் துணிந்தபின்
எண்ணுவம் என்பது இழுக்கு. (467)

Enni Thuniga Karumam Thuninthapin
Ennuvam Enpathu Izhukku

A better translation of this kural could be – Take up a decision only after a detailed assessment and it is wrong to regret a decision taken.

A Positive Thinker must take everything positively in his/her stride even if it turns out to be unfavorable and not regret a decision taken (if taken after a detailed assessment). Think twice before taking a decision but don't lament on a decision taken.

LOOK BEFORE YOU LEAP, LEARN FROM MISTAKES BUT NEVER LAMENT AFTER THE LEAP.

Cautious Optimism and Prudent Optimism

Definition of Cautious Optimism as per dictionary is – "A feeling of general confidence regarding a situation and/or its outcome coupled with readiness for possible difficulties or failure."

"If I advocate cautious optimism it is not because I do not have faith in the future but because I do not want to encourage blind faith."

– Aung San Suu Kyi

I would suggest that the phrase 'Prudent Optimism,' more than 'Cautious Optimism,' matches Positive Thinking closely.

Learning from Mistakes

A Positive Thinker looks back only to learn and not to lament. He/she learns from the mistakes and moves forward.

There is a beautiful and widely used term in Sanskrit called *simha-avalokanam* (सिंहावलोकन). Simha-avalokanam literally means 'Lion's backward look.' This can be roughly translated as introspection, recapitulation, etc.

Simha-avalokanam is the 'Lion's view of the path it treads.' A Lion stands atop a mound and assesses the path taken by him not for retracing but to prepare for the next leap. *Simha-avalokana-nyaya* maxim (the lion's looking back) is "looking back in order to leap ahead".

Can we add to the adage and complete it?

LOOK BEFORE YOU LEAP, LEARN FROM THE PREVIOUS LEAPS TO THE NEXT LEAP FORWARD. BUT, NEVER REGRET A LEAP MADE.

Take Aways

1. Look for opportunities in every challenge, pray for challenges.

2. 'Positive Thinking' and 'Negative Thinking' are infectious. Develop the company of 'Positive Thinkers' and shun the company of 'Negative Thinkers.'

3. Think 'Win-Win' strategies for every initiative.

4. Learn to be happy and accept any outcome.

5. Assess before taking any action, Learn from the actions in order to move forward but never lament on a decision taken.

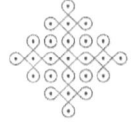

3. Procrastination, a Disease

Timely Action, a Virtue

Table 3: Literature References for Timely Action

Sl.	Illustration	Work	Reference	Author	Language	Remarks
1.	Kaalkare so aajkar	Kabir Doha		Sant Kabir	Hindi	
2.	Naalainaalai-enrerahil	Not known		Not known	Tamil	
3.	Thoonguha-thoongir	Thirukkural	672, Chapter 'Modes of Action'	Thiruvalluvar	Tamil	
4.	Shad doshaa	ViduraNiti (115)	prajāgaraparva – a subsection of the Udyoga Parva of the Mahabharata	Veda-vyasa	Sanskrit	Vidhura's advice to Dridarashtra

Greatest Evil Called Procrastination

One of the impediments for growth is an evil called *'procrastination.'* We normally get tempted to push things to the last minute. Whenever there is a deadline, tasks invariably get postponed close to the deadline and get into stress because of the pressure. Sounds familiar?

Do you pay your bills only on the last date? Do you have the habit of submitting your expense claims only after receiving a reminder from the finance team? Do you start preparing for your 'Income Tax Returns' only a day before the last date and still pray that the Income Tax department will give additional grace time for filing returns? Do you start working on an RFP response only two days before the last date? You surely are afflicted with the disease called 'procrastination.'

The disease 'procrastination' keeps you always in your time quadrant **'Urgent and Important Work'** and saps your energy from spending your precious time on **'Important but not Urgent'** work i.e., planning for the future.

I mentioned in the first Chapter, Hard Work never harms anyone, but stressful work does. A farmer who toils in the field for the most part of the day, lives 'hale, healthy and longer.' Stress from work affects health. Stress not only affects health but also affects the quality of work. Procrastination adds to stress.

I made a promise to myself to discuss only 'positive' things in this book. 'Procrastination' is not a 'positive' trait. Hence let us change the discussion topic to 'timely action.'

There is a beautiful Doha from Saint Kabir in Hindi.

काल करे सो आज कर, आज करै सो अब ।
पल में परलय होयगी, बहुरी करेगा कब ॥

Meaning of the Doha:

Finish tomorrow's tasks today;
And Today's tasks right now;
(Who knows), when you would finish them
If the world were to end in the next moment.

Procrastination is probably the root cause of all stress. Procrastination also makes us spend more energy than what is required to complete a job.

"Stress incurred, and the Energy spent in completing a task is directly proportional to the time difference between the time when the task was actually completed and the time when the task was ought to have been completed."

Stress ∞ Time when the task was completed – Time when the task was ought to have been completed.

Procrastinating a job pushes a job into the top left quadrant, i.e.,'Important and Urgent' leaving us limited time for the precious quadrant 'Important but Not Urgent' as per Stephen Covey's model of Time Management[1]

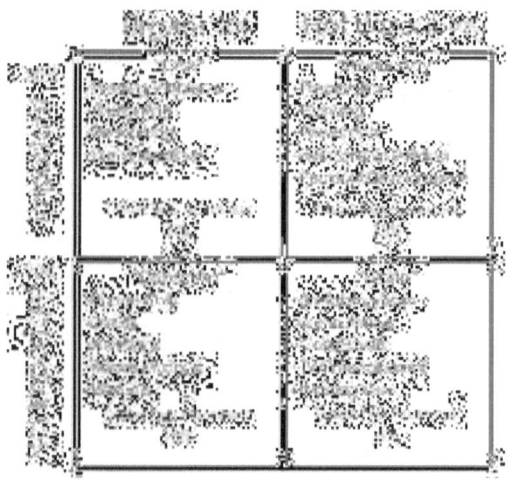

Figure 11: Stephen Covey's Time Management Matrix

---

[1]*Courtesy Time Management Matrix by Stephen Covey, author of 'The Seven Habits of Highly Effective People.'*

3. PROCRASTINATION, A DISEASE

"Efficient Time Management is the Discipline of doing what is important before it becomes Urgent."

This Tamil poem stresses the importance of 'timely completion' very nicely.

---

[1]Naalai naalaienreerahil Nammudai murainaal aavadumariyeer

Namanudai murainaal aavadumariyeer

Onre seiga onrum nanre seiga Inre seiga inrum inne seiga

Meaning – Don't procrastinate a task to tomorrow. We are not aware of our date with Lord Yama (God of Death). Need to complete a task with focus, that too with quality, that too on the same day and that too now. Focus on Work, Quality of Work and Timely completion—three important attributes for a task.

The Thirukkural given below also stresses the importance of completing tasks without delay.

தூங்குக தூங்கிச் செயற்பால தூங்கற்க
தூங்காது செய்யும் வினை *(672)*

Meaning of this kural is that the tasks which cannot be delayed should be completed immediately.

---

[1]*Very popular Tamil Poem but not able to find the author of the quoted Tamil poem.*

दीर्घसूत्रता (Dheergasutrata) is the right word for procrastination in Sanskrit. *Vidhura,* the younger brother of King *Dhritarashtra* in the epic *Mahabharata* offers sagacious advice to the King quite often in the epic Mahabharata. Advice from Vidhura includes many aspects of Dharma, Karma, etc. Vidura explains six faults that should be avoided.

षट् दोषाःपुरुषेणेहहातव्याभूतिमिच्छता ।
निद्रातन्द्राभयं क्रोधःआसस्यंदीर्घसूत्रता ॥ 115

Meaning – Six deficiencies found in this world are to be renounced by those who desire well-being and prosperity. Namely fondness for sleeping, lethargy, fearfulness, anger, laziness and procrastinating a task.

Take Aways

1. Complete a task when it is ought to have been completed with focus and this will ensure quality of work completion and reduced stress.

2. Complete the tasks when it is 'not urgent' so that you will always have enough time for 'urgent and important' activities.

4. Perseverance & Determination

Table 4: Literature References for 'Perseverance & Determination'

Sl.	Illustration	Work	Reference	Author	Language	Remarks
1.	Anirved-ahsriyo	ViduraNiti (72)	prajāgara parva – a subsection of the Udyoga Parva of the Mahabharata	Veda-vyasa	Sanskrit	Vidhura's advice to Dhrita-rashtra
2.	Arumaiu-daithenru	Thirukkural	611, Chapter – 'Manly Effort'	Thiruvalluvar	Tamil	
3.	Dhaivatha-nagathu	Thirukkural	619, Chapter – 'Manly Effort'	Thiruvalluvar	Tamil	
4.	Prarabh-yatenakalu	NitiSathak	Sloke 27	Raja Bhartruhari	Sanskrit	Referred as a subha-shitam
5.	Manadhiluru-dhivendum	Bharathiar Songs		Bharathiar	Tamil	Prayer Song
6.	I thought that my voyage had come to its end	Closed Path		Rabindranath Tagore	English	
7.	Aakamezhan-domenru	Thirukkural	593, Chapter – 'Energy'	Thiruvalluvar	Tamil	

Perseverance is a very powerful and useful attitude. Perseverance and Determination more or less refer to the same attitude. They are basically the drive to 'keep going' until the mission is achieved and 'not losing hope' when faced with difficulties.

What Is the Difference Between Perseverance and Determination?

Dictionary definition of Perseverance is doing something despite difficulty or delay in achieving success.

Dictionary definition of Determination is the ability to continue doing something, although it is very difficult.

Perseverance is used when one must endure extraordinary delays. Perseverance is used when one ought to make numerous attempts at something without losing hope.

Whereas the term Determination is associated mostly with courage, single-minded-focus, undeterred by failures, not worried about the obstacles, ambition against odds, etc.

I am greatly moved by this advice from *Vidura* on the positive aspects of Perseverance.

Vidura's advice is as follows:

anirvedaḥ śriyo mūlaṁ lābhasya śubhasya ca |
mahān bhavaty anirviṇṇaḥ sukhaṁ
cātyantam aśnute || 72

Figure 12: Vidhurar with Lord Krishna

The word *anirvedah* represents the trait of 'absence of dejection.' Perseverance is the root of prosperity, of profit and of what is beneficial. One who pursues a project with perseverance and without giving it up in vexation, is great, and enjoys unending happiness.

Tiruvalluvar, in this Thirukkural, has mentioned about Perseverance in a detailed manner.

Following few couplets will show how much importance he gave for this important quality everyone should imbibe:

அருமை உடைத்தென்று அசாவாமை வேண்டும்
பெருமை முயற்சி தரும். *(611)*

இது செய்வதற்கு அருமையாகாது என்று சோர்வுறாமல் இருக்க வேண்டும், அதைச் செய்வதற்குத்தக்க பெருமையை முயற்சி உண்டாக்கும்.

Meaning – Do not shy away or shun a task just because it is tough; perseverance brings the required energy to do the task and the respect of success.

தெய்வத்தான் ஆகா தெனினும் முயற்சிதன்
மெய்வருத்தக் கூலி தரும். *(619)*

ஊழியின் காரணத்தால் ஒரு செயல் செய்ய முடியாமல் போகுமாயினும், முயற்சி தன் உடம்பு வருந்திய வருத்தத்தின் கூலியையாவது கொடுக்கும்.

Meaning – Even if God has given up (which is unlikely), perseverance will give the fruits for one's efforts.

Ramanujar's 18 Journeys

Ramanujacharya is an accomplished vaishnavaite acharya. Refer PREFACE section for more details. Ramanuja demonstrated many leadership skills in his life of accomplishments.

Ramanujar's guru, *PeriaNambi,* advised him to learn *mahamantra* from another great *acharya, Thirukoshtiyur Nambi.* Ramanujar walked from Srirangam, where he was based, to Thirukoshtiyur where Thirukoshtiyur Nambi had his base (a distance of about 150 miles) by foot as many as 18 times before he could learn the *astaksharamantram* from Thirukoshtiyur Nambi. Thirukoshtiyur Nambi wanted to test Ramanujar's steadfastness as an eligibility to learn the esoteric truths and sent him back every time. Ramanujar never gave up until he learnt what he wanted to learn.

DETERMINATION is the ability to overcome certain dreadful fears, the following fears:

- Fear of failure
- Fear of difficulties
- Fear of circumstances

Determination can be best understood from this Sanskrit sloka from *Bhartrihari's NeetiShatak.*

प्रारभ्यतेनखलुविघ्नभयेननीचैः
प्रारभ्यविघ्ननिहताविरमन्तिमध्याः।
विघ्नैःपुनःपुनरपिप्रतिहन्यमानाः
प्रारब्धमुत्तमजनानपरित्यजन्ति॥

Transliteration of this is

Prarabyatena kalu vignabayena nichai
Prarabya vignanihata viramanti madhyah ।
Vignaih punahpunarapi pratihanyamanah
Prarabdham uttama janana parityajanti ॥

Translation of This Gem Is As Follows

Weak-minded people do not begin anything at all thinking about the fear of difficulties. Mediocre people begin work but abandon it when an obstacle comes their way, but strong-minded people though repeatedly hindered by difficulties do not give up what they have once begun.

Wake up with determination, Go to bed with satisfaction.

மனதிலுறுதி வேண்டும்,
வாக்கினிலேயினிமை வேண்டும்
– Bharathiyar

Tamil poet Bharathiyar prays for Determination and pleasing speech.

Fear of Failures

When one door gets closed, it is a signal from God that another door will open, leading to a better path.

> When one door closes, another opens; but we often look so long and so regretfully upon the closed door that we do not see the one which has opened for us.
>
> – Alexander Graham Bell

> "Our greatest glory is not in never failing, but in rising every time we fail".
>
> – Confucious

If Thomas Edison had been afraid of failure, we would still be living in darkness. If Henry Ford had given up, we would still be riding on horseback. If Alexander Graham Bell had given in to the clutches of failure we would still have been sending messages through pigeons.

A lot can be learnt from Tagore's poem on 'Not Giving Up' and 'Getting Back Up after setbacks.'

> I thought that my voyage had come to its end at the last limit of my power, that the path before me was closed, that provisions were exhausted and the time come to take shelter in silent obscurity, but I find that thy will knows no end in me, and when old words die out on the tongue, new melodies break forth from the heart, and where the old tracks are lost, new country is revealed with its wonders.
>
> – Rabindranath Tagore

This is best illustrated from this real-life incident from the biography of Dr. Kalam.

People's President Dr. APJ Abdul Kalam was a very successful man in his life and made India proud with successes in ISRO and DRDO. Do you know that Kalam failed in his maiden attempt at seeking his career and failed to achieve his dream? But, he overcame his setback and left an inspirational message for all. He showed everyone how to learn from failures.

Dr. Kalam's 'dearest dream' was to become a fighter pilot. He attended an interview for fighter pilot at IAF, Dehradun and missed it by a whisker. Dr. Kalam bagged the ninth position out of 25 candidates and was not recruited as only eight slots were available. Kalam was deeply disappointed. Such was the disappointment that he trekked from Dehradun to Rishikesh, distance of 50 kilometers. He was wandering around the hills at Rishikesh when he happened to meet Swami Shivanand—a Muslim boy meeting a Hindu seer. Swami Shivanand comforted him, "Accept your destiny and go ahead with your life. You are not destined to serve in the air force. What you are destined to become is not revealed now, but it is predetermined. Forget this failure, as it is essential to lead you to your destined path." Kalam respected the advice and joined Directorate of Technical Development and Production (DTD&P-Air) of the Defense Ministry at Delhi, went on to steer rockets, missiles and a nuclear bomb.

Dr. Kalam mentions in his book, "I hope these stories will help all my readers understand their dreams and compel them to work on these dreams that keep them awake." We will have to add, "Don't get deterred by the failures when pursuing your dream; probably they are the indications that you are destined to do something better."

Dr. Kalam's very interesting quotes on Failures:

If you **FAIL**, it is **F**irst **A**ttempt **I**n **L**earning.

There is no **END** to sincere efforts, **E**ffort **N**ever **D**ies.

If you encounter **NO** as an answer, don't worry, there is always **N**ext **O**pportunity.

It doesn't matter how many times you fall; what counts is how many times you stand up again.

Fear of Difficulties – Main Khelega

Figure 13: Sachin Tendulkar

This is the heroic story of a 16-year-old wonder boy. Yes. I am talking about the famous cricketer, Sachin Tendulkar.

Sachin Tendulkar made his debut against Pakistan on November 15, 1989. Tendulkar was all of 16 years and 205 days old when he was brought in to play against the ferocious fast bowling trio of Waqar Younis, Wasim Akram and Imran Khan. In the first test match, Tendulkar got out early, clean bowled by Younis for 15 runs. In the second match, however, he slammed 59 runs and hit every Pakistan bowler for fours. However, the main showdown was reserved for the fourth Test match. India was in a disadvantageous position in all the three tests and managed to salvage draws in all the three matches.

The pitch at Sialkot for the fourth and final test was prepared conducive for the fast bowlers. Pakistani fans had huge expectations. Waqar did not disappoint the fans. In the first innings, Tendulkar made a well composed 35, batting with his two fingers strapped, after being hit by the bouncer. India was four down for 38 runs in the second innings. Navjot Singh Sidhu was at the crease when Tendulkar walked in to bat.

Looking at the obnoxiously rising balls, Sidhu was worried about the fate of the 16-year-old kid. Sidhu explains the scenario in his own gregarious style.

Waqar Younis came in to bowl and slammed the ball in the middle of the wicket. The ball hit squarely on Tendulkar's nose. He was bleeding profusely. Blood came gushing down on his gears. Indian physio, Ali Irani, ran towards him for help. Non-striker Navjot Singh Sidhu also ran to his rescue. When everybody was waiting for Sachin Tendulkar to be carried out on a stretcher, he spoke those two words in his quirky voice and broken Hindi that defined his character, "*main khelega*." Sidhu was flabbergasted. Tendulkar continued to bat with his badgered nose. Sidhu comments in his speech, "If I had got hurt like that, I would have gone to sleep until the end of the match, leave alone playing," and continues, "Looking at the grit of the 16-year-old boy, I got motivated to fight and managed to score 97 and drew the match". Gritty Tendulkar got up and hit the next ball by Waqar Younis for four runs.

And after that, Sachin did exactly what he said. He played for the next 23 years and made every record possible in world cricket for a batsman. He has 100 centuries in international cricket. He is the leading run scorer in both Test matches and ODI matches. He became the God of cricket. But it all started with those two words. 'Main Khelega' meaning "I WILL PLAY (come what may)."

"He's 40, but there hasn't been a single day when he has not given it his all, be it in the nets or during a match" his teammates remembered during his retirement.

You have to be a believer first, and you will become an achiever. Sachin Tendulkar laid an example not only for the sportsmen but also for all of us. There will be times when problems will be thrown at us making our life difficult. There will be times when obstacles will knock us down on our face. **Stand up and say, "I will play,"** stare at the obstacle and say, **"I will not get cowed down."**

Fear of Circumstances – FIGHTING AGAINST ODDS

Let us see a few incredible Indian stories.

The story of Swapna Barman, the 21-year-old gold medal winner in the heptathlon event at the recently concluded Asian Games is one of grit and determination. The daughter of a rickshaw-puller and tea-estate worker from the remote town Jalpaiguri in West Bengal, Swapna was born with 12 toes and has had a difficult time dealing with this condition all her life. She overcame physical pain and discomfort to become the first Indian woman to win gold in the heptathlon, which is a track-and-field combination of seven different events: 100-meters hurdles, high jump, shot put, 200 meters, long jump, javelin throw, and 800 meters. She accrued a total of 6,026 points over two days, giving close competition to and finally defeating her accomplished Chinese counterpart, Qingling Wang. She requires custom-made shoes to accommodate the extra toes, but she could not afford the cost of special shoes. She endured pain and struggles to reach her dream. The pain did not deter her from dreaming. She dreamt big and fought against the odds. She explains this in her own words:

"I was always dismissed by officials and critics who ridiculed me by saying I am too short and fat for heptathlon, and that I can't go beyond 5,600–5,700 points."

She did not get perturbed and proved everyone wrong by accruing 6,026 points. Her dream did not stop with the Asian Games. Her dream in her own words:

Figure 14: Swapna Burman at Asaid 2018

"I now plan to get over 6,200 points in the world championship that can give me a medal. But the ultimate aim is an Olympic Medal, which is a realistic possibility. That no longer is a distant dream."

"Every Finishing Line Is a New Starting Line."

– Mahatria

Looking at her determination, I am sure her dream of winning an Olympic Medal will come through.

Here is another extraordinary tale of grit and determination that took the son of an alcoholic from Melaottankadu village in Pattukottai in Thanjavur district to the platforms of the St. Thomas Mount Railway Station and the hallways of IIT Madras enroute to his dream of becoming an IAS officer. M. Sivaguru Prabakaran gave up his dream of pursuing an engineering degree as his family couldn't afford the money. After this, is the story of poverty, hard work, perseverance and a 'never say die' attitude. An alcoholic father meant that much of the earning burden fell on his mother and sister who made ends meet weaving coconut fronds. When he couldn't pursue engineering, he decided to work to support the family. Sivaguru worked as a mill operator, a farm laborer, and later as an engineer. After spending money for his family, he saved some to pursue his dream of becoming an IAS officer.

During his training for IIT, Sivaguru, for close to four months, used to sleep in the St. Thomas Mount Railway Station. He used to travel by train and reach on Saturday, attend classes on Saturday and Sunday, staying at the railway station platform for the night. This went on till he found a friend in his coaching class who was ready to share a room with him.

"There is no hurdle that can't be broken. I used to hit every obstacle harder and harder till it broke. Perseverance and hard work will take everyone a long way."

– Sivaguru

Figure 15: Sivaguru Prabhakaran

On his fourth attempt, Sivaguru cleared his UPSC with All India Rank 101. He says that constant preparation and an urge to serve the public is what helped him achieve this success. From a small village to finishing engineering and then IIT with a 9.0 GPA to cracking the UPSC, this villager is an inspiration for hundreds of people now. He did not give up and exploited the power of his subconscious mind to achieve his dream.

Lack of Resourcefulness and Not Resources

When he was born, neighbors in the village suggested that his parents smother him. It was better than the pain they would have to go through their lifetime, some said. He is a useless baby without eyes.

Srikanth Bolla is now living by his conviction that, "If the world looks at me and says, 'Srikanth, you can do nothing,' I look back at the world and say I can do anything."

Srikanth Bolla was born blind into a family of farmers in rural India and went on to become the first international blind student at MIT. Bolla chose to return to India where he set up Bollant Industries in Hyderabad, a company that employs and trains differently-abled individuals to manufacture eco-friendly and compostable packaging. The company has been a recent recipient of an undisclosed investment funding from Ratan Tata believed to be around $1.3 million. Bolla is already into Forbes List of '30 under 30 – Asia.'

Srikanth considers himself the luckiest man alive, not because he is now a millionaire, but because his uneducated parents, who earned Rs. 20,000 a year, did not heed any of the advice they received and raised him with love and affection. "They are the richest people I know," says Srikanth.

Figure 16: Srikanth Bolla, Founder of Bollant Industries

Srikanth's success did not come just like that. He had to fight his way to the top. He was denied admission into Science stream at Class XI because he was blind. He had to fight a case in the court to get admission. He was not allowed to write the IIT entrance exam. He did his homework through the Internet and got admission to MIT, Stanford, Berkeley, and Carnegie Mellon. He went to MIT with a scholarship as the first international blind student in the school's history.

After completing his stint at MIT, Srikanth decided to give up the 'golden' opportunity in corporate America and came back to India in search of his dream. He set up a support service platform to rehabilitate, nurture and integrate differently-abled people in society. Then he built Bollant to give employment for the trained differently-abled people, and Bollant now employs 150 differently-abled people.

Bollant's co-founder Swarnalatha was his special needs teacher at the school. She trains all the employees with disabilities at Bollant thereby creating a strong community where they feel valued. Swarnalatha adds, "Srikanth is a true source of my inspiration. He is not only my young friend and protégé but is also my mentor who teaches me daily that **anything is possible if you set your mind to it.**"

Srikanth is a true source of inspiration for all of us.

It's not the lack of resources, it's your lack of resourcefulness that stops you.

– Tony Robbins

Not everyone starts his/her career with money, privilege, or connections. Some people make their fortunes by finding a need and filling it. The Steves (Jobs and Wozniak, of Apple) started with little more than resourcefulness and a dream. It's far easier to throw out excuses and live a mediocre life. But I think that with a little resourcefulness and a dream to drive you forward, anyone can make something wonderful happen.

Thiruvalluvar's kural 593 would have been the motivation for Swapnas and Sivagurus.

ஆக்கம் இழந்தேமென்று அல்லாவார் ஊக்கம்
ஒருவந்தம் கைத்துடை யார். *(593)*

This kural means, "Those who are highly motivated, even if they lose all their possessions, will never feel desperate."

"If opportunity doesn't knock, build a door."

– Milton Berle

Lots of opportunities come knocking if we are receptive. The trick is to recognize them. Then you must decide whether or not to open the door.

I would like to conclude the discussion on this interesting attitude with my favorite quote from Mahakavi Bharathiyar

கண் திறந்திட வேண்டும்,

காரியத்தில் உறுதி வேண்டும்;

KaNthiRandhidavaeNdum,

KaariyathiluRuthivaeNdum;

HAVE A VISION. STAY DETERMINED IN WHATEVER YOU DO.

Take Aways

1. Never ever give up.

2. Practice to overcome the fears – Fear of failures, Fear of difficulties and Fear of circumstances.

3. When one door gets closed, look for other open doors instead of continuing to look regretfully at the closed door.

4. Wake up with determination and go to bed with satisfaction.

5. When you face an obstacle in your life, stare at the obstacle and say 'I will overcome.'

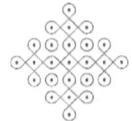

5. Dream Big

Table 5: Literature References for 'Dreaming Big'

Sl.	Illustration	Work	Reference	Author	Language	Remarks
1.	Sindhu nadhiinmisai	Bharathiyar Songs		Bharathiyar	Tamil	National Integration Song
2.	Vellathania-neermattam	Thirukkural	595, Chapter 'Energy'	Thiruvalluvar	Tamil	
3.	Thammir-periyar	Thirukkural	444, Chapter 'Seeking the aid of great men'	Thiruvalluvar	Tamil	
4.	Kani nilamvendum	Bharathiyar Songs		Bharathiyar	Tamil	
5.	Nunnia-noolpala	Thirukkural	373, Chapter 'Fate'	Thiruvalluvar	Tamil	

Everyone dreams. I get wild dreams invariably every night since childhood! They are not called dreams. Shall we call them 'nightmares' to reserve apt definition for 'Dreaming big'?

"Dream is not that which you see in sleep. It is something that does not let you sleep."

– People's President Dr. APJ Abdul Kalam.

We can learn the power of an apt dream from the famous '*I have a Dream*' speech by Martin Luther King, Jr. delivered on August 28, 1963 at the Lincoln Memorial, Washington DC. This is considered the greatest demonstration for freedom in the history of the USA. Former President Barack Obama quoted this dream as his inspiration. Powerful dreams can be an inspiration for many.

Bharathiyar's Dream

Has dreaming been eulogized in Indian Literature? Yes, copiously. Let us take an example of a powerful dream from Tamil poet, Subramanya Bharati.

Like Thiruvalluvar, Bharati was also a versatile poet. He composed songs on a variety of subjects—Indian Freedom Movement, His love for Tamil language, National Integration, Women Empowerment, Devotion, Love, Kids, leaders and leadership what not? His specialty is the passion in his poems. This song '*Bharata Desam*' is an excellent example to understand the power of 'Dreaming.'

சிந்து நதியின் மிசை நிலவினிலே
சேரநன்னாட்டிளம் பெண்களுடனே
சுந்தரத் தெலுங்கினில் பாட்டிசைத்து
தோணிகளோட்டி விளையாடி வருவோம்

This is a famous song by Bharathiyar and has been used in many movies. Bharathiyar is a *vaggeyakarar,* meaning he set the tune (raga) himself for many of his

songs. This song was set in the raga *'punnagavarali.'*
This song primarily talks about the power of National
Integration and covers every region of Modern India.
He starts from the beauty of River Sindhu, Beauty of
Kerala womenfolk, the sweetness of Telugu language
(important to remember here that he is the one who said
Tamil is the sweetest of all the languages he knew of),
Poetic beauty of Marathi poets, etc. A more interesting
aspect of this poem is his 'vision' for Independent India
espoused in these lines:

சிங்களத் தீவினுக்கோர் பாலமமைப்போம்
சேதுவை மேடுறுத்தி விதி சமைப்போம்.
வங்கத்தில் ஓடி வரும் நீரின் மிகையால்
மையத்து நாடுகளில் பயிர் செய்குவோம்

Translation of This Stanza – Let us build a bridge to Sri
Lanka and make Sethusamudram Pass a commercial hub
between India and Sri Lanka. Let us use the excess water
from the rivers in Bengal to irrigate crops in Central parts
of India. What a powerful dream? Remember that Bharati
compiled this song in 1910 when India was still ruled
by the British who had no vision for a Developed India.
India in those days used to be considered by many as a
conglomeration of diverse land and people of different
culture. Every freedom fighter dreamt about Independent
India. Bharati went many steps ahead and dreamt about a
Free India, Integrated India and a Powerful well developed
India.

Our politicians are still talking about Interlinking of Rivers, 97 years after his death. We still don't have any plan for building a bridge to Sri Lanka. Channel Tunnel, the most popular underwater tunnel, is a 50.45-kilometer rail tunnel linking Folkestone, Kent, in the United Kingdom, with Coquelles, Pas-de-Calais, near Calais in northern France, beneath the English Channel at the Strait of Dover. Channel Tunnel was opened on 6th May 1994, 73 years after Bharathiyar died. Bharathiyar dreamt about a bridge across Sethusamudram much before Channel Tunnel was even conceptualized.

Did he think about the difficulty in building a bridge between India and Sri Lanka and interlinking Bengal rivers with Central Indian rivers? A visionary does not get limited by the 'viability of his dream,' nor by the 'scale of difficulty.' A visionary believes strongly that his dream will fructify however difficult and far-sighted it may be.

வானையளப்போம் கடல்மீ னையளப்போம்
சந்திரமண்டலத்தியல்கண்டு தெளிவோம்

These lines also form part of the same song. Here, he dreams about advances in Astronomy, using technology to measure the concentration of fishes in ocean and Space Technology to the moon. India mastered these technologies but these were not heard of during Bharathiyar's time. He had elucidated that technology was to be used for common man's good. Even Apollo 8 the first space manned mission to enter the moon's orbit was launched in December 1968, 58 years after Bharathi wrote this song.

DREAM BIG

Let us see how Thiruvalluvar advised us to think big. Meaning of this kural is the same as the Management philosophy *'Attitude determines Altitude.'*

வெள்ளத் தனைய மலர்நீட்டம் மாந்தர்தம்
உள்ளத் தனையது உயர்வு. *(595)*

Transliteration (Tamil to English):

vellath thanaiya malarnheettam maandhardham
ullath thanaiya dhuuyarvu

Meaning – A water flower raises its stem when the water level rises. Similarly, the degree of achievement is dependent upon the 'thoughts' of an Individual.

To put it simply, Positive Attitude is the key to Better Life. Think big and you will rise higher.

Auto Anna's Big Thinking

An auto driver from Chennai, a class 12 dropout, is now a much sought-after motivational speaker in corporate circles. His speech went viral on YouTube. Yes. Annadurai a.k.a. Auto Anna has already given two TED talks and talked to the employees of 40 corporate giants like Vodafone, Hyundai, Royal Enfield, etc. His rise is a perfect example of the above Thirukkural.

What Does He Do for His Living?

Annadurai drives a 'share auto' which can carry five to six people on Old Mahabalipuram Road (OMR), Chennai where most of the IT companies are located. What has he achieved big to deserve such acclaim? **He dreamt big and achieved high.** He dreamt big in a way no one imagined. He made his auto Wi-Fi enabled and equipped his auto with a TV set, laptop, tablet and iPad—the latter three devices being available for customers who like to do some browsing as they travel. He plays the day's important news clips on the TV set, which he normally records during lunch break at home. He also keeps a stock of popular film songs from major Indian Languages and plays them for customers from other states who like to hear songs in their native tongue. He keeps a collection of eight dailies and the latest issues of not less than 35 magazines that are stacked neatly inside the auto. He installed card swiping machine so that his customers can pay through their credit card!

Annadurai also offers free or discounted rides on special days. Teachers are offered free rides daily, lovers on Valentine's Day, and women traveling with their children on Mother's Day. He earns around Rs. 45,000 every month and spends from it about Rs. 9,000 on the various amenities he provides for his customers. He has an interesting website (http://www.amazingauto.in/). For the moment, he is preparing for the launch of an app that would enable his customers to track the movement of his auto, check seat availability and book a ride.

Figure 17: Auto Annadurai

Auto Anna dreamt big when most of his other peers stayed back worrying about the dwindling revenues because of the onslaught of *Ola* and *Uber*. Auto Anna retained and improved his loyal customer base because of his Big Thinking.

The first step towards becoming a 'big thinker' involves incorporating the habit of thinking big in every aspect of your life. Thinking big requires that you see things from a wider and far-reaching perspective.

One must fantasize to think big—childlike fantasy. Think like a child, who has a curious nature and only sees possibilities. A child does not calculate probabilities. In order to think big, you must think from the perspective of having no limitations and no fears. Think as if life is conspiring in your favor, breaking down all the obstacles. Develop the habit of thinking big, acting big, and doing bigger things than you ever thought were possible.

Those who think big ask Big questions consistently and persistently until the right answer comes to mind. They ask questions like:

- How can I do this better than anyone else?

- How can I think more creatively about this?

- How can I take this to another level?

- How can I think even bigger?

Their thinking does not get limited by questions such as:

- Is it possible?

- Is it achievable?

Dream Impossible. Make Your Dreams Inevitable by Your Actions.

This Thirukkural (596) substantiates the advice that the thinking need not get limited to feasibility. What will happen if you 'think big' but not able to achieve.

உள்ளுவ தெல்லாம் உயர்வுள்ளல் மற்றது
தள்ளினுந் தள்ளாமை நீர்த்து. 596

Meaning of This Thirukkural: Always Think Big. Continue to think even if you are not able to achieve due to fate. You will still be appreciated, and this is a victory.

To dream big, surround yourself with people who themselves dream big.

> To develop your *Ego* surround yourself with those who look up to you. To develop *Yourself* surround yourself with those you look up to.
>
> – Mahatria Ra

This reminds me the Thirukkural 444

தம்மிற் பெரியார் தமரா ஒழுகுதல்
வன்மையுளெல்லாந் தலை. *444*

Meaning: Be in the company of and be guided by people who are greater than you in knowledge and other attributes. This is the greatest strength.

How to Dream?

Bharathiyar compiled one more song on Dreaming, this time to explain the process of Dreaming. Yes. What modern management gurus say about Dreaming Big.

Dreaming is only the first step. *What Next?* We don't dream just for the fun of dreaming. We dream obviously to realize the dreams. The following seven steps are suggested as tips on 'How to Dream and How to achieve your Dreams.'

- **Dream It. Dream It Big.** Every great achievement began with a Dream and strong belief that it was possible. Don't let negative thinking or negative comments from others discourage you.

- **Believe in Your Dream.** Think Big. Dreams need not be limited by 'practicality.' But it must be believable. Develop a strong belief that the dream is achievable.

- **Visualize Your Dream.** Detail your dream. Great achievers develop the habit of visualizing their dreams. Picture your dreams. **Example:** If you dream of being an entrepreneur, imagine yourself sitting in the CEO's chair in a posh corporate office and chairing a powerful Board Meeting. If you aspire to become a cricket star, imagine yourself hitting a huge sixer in a T20 match for India playing an in-swinger from James Anderson. If you dream for a coveted award, picture yourself receiving the award from your favorite dignitary in the Ballroom of Taj Palace hotel to the thunderous applause from the audience. Fantasize. Fantasize like a child. Details are very important in your visualization.

- **Bring Your Passion to the Dream or Make It Your Passion.** Associate your dream to a few things you are passionate about in your life and/ormake your dream as the passion for you in your life.

- **Share Your Dreams.** Share your dreams with your well-wishers, near and dear and people whom you look upto. Don't be shy of sharing your dreams. Don't worry about what others would think of you. As we share with more people, we begin to believe it more and more. When we tell more, it makes us accountable and stimulates us to act.

- **Take Some Action Every Day.** Take 'baby steps' towards realizing your dreams but do it on a daily basis. Start your day thinking about what could be done during the day and end the day thinking about what has been done for the day. Make this a daily routine. Consistent action is more important than sporadic exuberance.

- **Assess Your Progress.** Look back and assess your progress periodically.

These seven aspects can guarantee success. Bharathiyar demonstrated steps 1 to 5 in his song *"Kani nilam vendum."* This is a favorite song for music lovers too.

On the outset, this song looks like a prayer song. Bharathiyar wrote this as a prayer to Goddess Parashakthi asking for a piece of land and a building on the land to live. But, the song is his dream to own a building of his liking. Please note here that Bharathiyar lived his life in penury without owning a permanent dwelling, moving from one place to another, constantly on the run from British Police. The beauty of this song is in 'How he visualizes and expresses his dream.' Let us enjoy the song and the lessons from the song.

காணிநிலம் வேண்டும் பராசக்தி காணிநிலம் வேண்டும்
அங்குத்தூணில் அழகிய தாய் நன்மாடங்கள் துய்ய
நிறத்தினவாய் அந்தக்காணி நிலத்திடையே
ஒர் மாளிகை கட்டித் தரவேண்டும் அங்குக்
கேணியருகினிலே தென்னைமரம் கீற்றும் இளநீரும்

பத்துப் பன்னிரெண்டு தென்னைமரம் பக்கத்திலே
வேணும் நல்ல முத்துச் சுடர் போலே நிலா வொளி
முன்பு வரவேணும் அங்குக் கத்தும் குயிலோசை
சற்றே வந்து காதிற்பட வேணும் என்றன் சித்தம்
மகிழ்ந்திடவே நன்றாய் இளந்தென்றல் வரவேணும்

பாட்டுக் கலந்திடவே அங்கே ஒரு பத்தினிப்பெண்
வேணும் எங்கள் கூட்டுக்களியினிலே கவிதைகள்
கொண்டு தரவேணும் அந்தக்காட்டு வெளியினிலே
அம்மா நின்றன் காவலுறவேணும் என்றன் பாட்டுத்
திறத்தாலே இவ்வையத்தைப்பாலித்திட வேணும்

The meaning of the above-mentioned lyrics is given below for those who do not understand the Tamil language (though poetic beauty can be enjoyed well in the native language only).

1. Oh Goddess Parashakthi, give me a piece of land of one *kaani* (kaani is the measure used for lands during Bharathiyar's time, measures about 1.32 acres), and there, in the midst of that small piece of land, you should build me a palace with ornate pillars and several floors of beautiful colors and there, near the well, coconut trees should shine with tender coconuts.

   Bharathiyar dreams big and picturizes his dream with all the associated details.

   Picturization continues further in the second stanza.

2. There should be ten to twelve coconut trees near the house.

   Moonlight should shine like a pearl,

   And the soft song of the cuckoos should caress my ears to make my mind happy.

   The light breeze should add to my happiness.

   He has covered every possible detail of his dream, i.e., owning a place to live, like what a modern-day realtor would specify (Only thing he probably missed is the dimension of the well ☺☺)

3. There should be a virtuous wife, to add music to my life,

   And our play together, should give birth to poems,

And in that forest-like expanse, Oh mother you should provide safety,

And my poetic expertise should help the world to live happily.

Bharathiyar's passion was writing poems. He associated his passion with his dream of owning a house. He dreamt about a life partner with whom he can share his passion in his dream house. Look at his self-confidence on his capabilities as a kavi. Thus, he has very well covered steps 1 to 5 as mentioned in the 'How to dream' section.

How does the picturization help with realizing the dream? Giving as much detail as possible to the powerful sub-conscious mind will help in realizing the dream(s). How?

"She is our own, the darling, of our hearts, Santiniketan,

Our dreams are rocked in her arms,

Her face is a fresh wonder of love every time we see her,

For she is our own, the darling of our hearts."

– Gurudev Rabindranath Tagore

Power of Sub-Conscious Mind

The subconscious mind is connected to 'dreams' as well as 'nightmares.' Our subconscious mind is responsible for the nightmares, and we can use the power of our subconscious mind to realize our dreams.

What Is Sub-Conscious Mind?

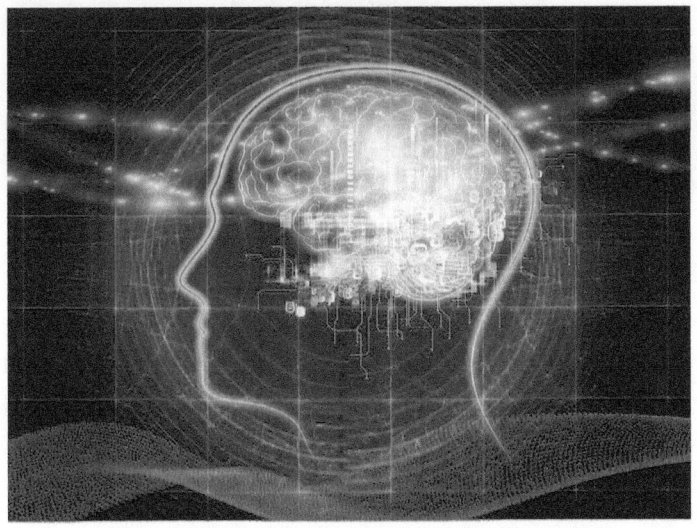

Figure 18: Subconscious Mind

Our mind is not as rational as we think. According to psychologists, the mind can be divided into three levels—Conscious, Subconscious and Unconscious (Some add the fourth Super Conscious level).

1. **Conscious**—Defines all thoughts and actions within our awareness. For example, the beauty and pleasant smell of rose. This is **logical and rational**.

2. **Subconscious**—Internalizes all reactions and automatic actions we can become aware of, if we think about them. For example, once we get skilled in driving a car, we stop thinking which gears to

use, which pedals to press, or which mirror to look at, yet can always become aware of what was done once we think about it.

3. **Unconscious**—defines all past events and memories, inaccessible to us no matter how hard we try to remember to bring things up. For example, the first word we've learned to say, or how it felt to be able to walk on our own.

Your Subconscious Mind Is Your Autopilot. Your ambitions and desires for the future are also stored in your subconscious mind.

When I tried playing the violin, for the first few attempts, I had to always keep looking at the string and which position the finger had to be kept playing the right *swaram*. It will be complete *abaswaram* the moment I take my focus out of the instrument. This is acquiring the skill at the conscious stage. Once I mastered the skill of playing the violin, I no longer needed to measure the finger's position. This is the subconscious mind in action.

Most likely, first attempts to synchronize a new set of complex actions are always difficult. Once we become more skilled, these movements start to require less conscious awareness until everything begins to flow naturally.

Conscious thoughts are processed slower than unconscious thoughts. The conscious mind is a rational mind and works based on good and bad, right and wrong. In contrast, the subconscious mind works based on deep and shallow emotions. Faith and belief are the foundation of the subconscious. Another important aspect is that the subconscious mind might not respond to force.

Power of sub-conscious mind was the invention of modern-day psychologists. But I was flabbergasted to read that Thiruvalluvar compiled a kural to describe the power of sub-conscious mind!!

Thiruvalluvar, in kural 373, describes the power of the subconscious mind.

நுண்ணிய நூல்பல கற்பினும் மற்றுந்தன்
உண்மை யறிவே மிகும்.   குறள் 373

The inner meaning of this kural is that, "A person's values are determined more by destiny (collection of thoughts) rather than his knowledge," which means, "Actions are based on the collection of thoughts, and the knowledge is bound to take the back seat." Psychologists concur with Thiruvalluvar that, "A person is prone to respond to situations based on their preconceived notions even if it is prejudiced." In 95% of the cases, academic knowledge is less likely to influence their response. This is where the subconscious mind takes precedence over the conscious mind.

There is a famous Sanskrit quote "यद्भावंतद्भवति" (Yad bhavam Tad bhavathi) which simply means "As you think so you become," i.e., your thoughts shape your destiny.

That is why our forefathers advised us to always think 'good.'

The subconscious mind is more powerful than the conscious mind. There are differing opinions on how powerful the subconscious mind is over the conscious mind. But all researchers agree that the subconscious mind is exponentially powerful than the conscious mind. While the conscious mind can just focus on a few things at a time, the subconscious mind can do so many things at the same time including collecting more information and processing more things. This makes it much easier for the subconscious mind to control your mood, emotions, perception and almost everything.

Our sub-conscious mind is so powerful that it will find ways and means of achieving our dream if we program our sub-conscious mind suitably.

You will be able to consciously give instructions to your subconscious mind instead of letting it control you. The ultimate form of power can happen when both your conscious and subconscious minds cooperate in such a way that they work towards the achievement of your goals.

Trees Cursing Magic

I don't know if there is a scientific explanation for this, but it is believed that the tribals of Solomon Islands use the technique of 'curse magic' to cut big trees, which are too big to be chopped down. They surround the tree and curse it for hours every day. Within a few weeks, the tree dries up and becomes dead. Many of us might find this example too difficult to believe. How can intangible and invisible thoughts and words kill a tree?

When the tribal of Solomon Islands curse a tree, they are actually instilling negative and harmful beliefs in the tree's emotion (yes, trees do have emotions too). Within a few days, the negative emotions become a belief, and eventually, changes the molecular structure of the tree, and slowly kills it from inside.

If this is the fate of the trees, we human beings can understand how powerful our **feelings are**. If you are constantly finding faults in the name of 'constructive criticism,' you are instilling beliefs in their mind that will keep harming them forever. If you keep appreciating them in a sincere way, you are instilling beliefs in their mind that will help them all their life.

Be careful of what you keep saying to yourself. Repetition of words and thoughts is the best way to develop a belief in your subconscious mind. If you keep saying you are a loser, don't be surprised if you become one within a few months or years. If you have friends who keep saying such things to you, there is no harm in telling a quick goodbye to them.

[1]Miracle Man

The story of Morris E. Goodman, an iron-willed, self-made salesman, known as 'Miracle Man' is highly motivational. This story is used as the training material for motivation. Morris suffered paralyzing injuries in a plane crash and used the power of his subconscious mind to achieve full recovery.

Morris Goodman was a successful insurance salesman. So successful, he bought his own airplane. On March 10, 1981, during the first solo flight in his new craft, the engine stopped, and he crashed the plane, crushing his spine, leaving him unable to walk, talk, swallow, breathe or move any part of his body except

---

[1]Courtesy http://www.themiracleman.org/index2.htm. *Read his book The Miracle Man: An Inspiring Story of Motivation and Courage for more details.*

his eyes. His doctors believed he would live a short, meaningless life if he survived at all. Morris had different plans. His family knew that he enjoyed Zig Ziglar and his philosophy of life, so they brought in a tape recorder and played Ziglar's tapes and inspirational messages over and over again for Morris. He decided to focus on willing himself to move his eye and one of his fingers. He spent three weeks visualizing himself moving his finger and winking his eye. Then, one day, when the nurse was in the room, he was able to wink his eye and the next day he moved his finger. What Morris had was his mind and his faith that one day he would walk out on his feet and make a full recovery. Morris began to calculate the steps he needed to make towards his recovery. He set a goal to be home by Christmas of that same year. He succeeded before Thanks giving, just eight months after the accident.

Our body responds to our thoughts!!

Focus on what you desire for your life. Say it positively and repeat it to yourself as often during the day as you can. For example, if you want to start a business, say, "I am happily working in my ideal business." When you declare what you want, you're making a promise to yourself, and your powerful subconscious mind will find ways to achieve your goal for you.

Few recommendations to help you use your subconscious power for your best:

1. Before going to bed, refer your wish to your subconscious mind, you will see its miraculous power in action. You can make a conscious connection to your subconscious mind.

2. Watch closely the thoughts and ideas governing your mind. Tune your thoughts to what you want to become.

3. When you have a specific goal or dream, consciously repeat this statement: "I believe that the power of the subconscious, which gave me this desire, will embody it in me now."

4. Cultivate in your subconscious mind **thoughts of health, peace and harmony,** and all the functions of the body will return to normal.

5. Fill your subconscious mind with the expectations of best experiences and emotions, and your thoughts will become a reality.

Imagine a positive outcome of your problems and fully feel the enthusiasm from what has happened. All your fantasies and feelings are clearly accepted by your subconscious and then implemented in life.

काममया एवायं पुरुष इति
सा यथाकामो भवति तत्क्रतुर भवति
यात्क्रतुर भवति तत कर्म कुरुते
यत कर्म कुरुते तद अभिसम पद्यते

You are what your deep, driving desire is
As your desire is, so is your will
As your will is, so is your deed
As your deed is, so is your destiny

Brihadaranyaka Upanishad, 4.4.5

Take Aways

1. Think big, Dream big.

2. Visualise your dreams and detail it.

3. Keep sharing your dreams with your near and dear.

4. Tune your subconscious mind to achieve your dreams.

5. Nurture good and positive thoughts. Practice gratitude for the past and ambition for the future.

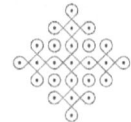

Section B

Five Springboarding Skills

Every skill you acquire doubles your odds of success.

– Scott Adams

कौशलस्य पञ्च प्रकाराः

ஐந்து திறமைகள்

योग: कर्मसुकौशलं
(Bhagavad Gita Chapter 2 Verse 50)

Here Lord Krishna says, "Skillful approach to performing an action is Yoga." One who handles his/her work skillfully can be called a yogic.

Skills require practice to perfect. Still, the starting point to acquire a skill is a positive attitude. Five skills that I found reference of in literature are:

1. Learning

2. Listening

3. Process Excellence

4. Communication Skill

5. Team Work

Many of the above five could be captured under **Attitudes** as well.

Acquiring Knowledge is a skill, but Learnability is an Attitude. Listening is a skill but requires an attitudinal change to perfect the listening skill. Process Orientation is also an Attitude. Perfecting Communication Skills require attitudinal change. Team Work starts with the attitude. For that matter, attitudinal change is the starting point for acquiring any skill.

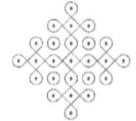

1. Unleash the Potential of Learning

Table 6: Literature References for 'Learning'

Sl.	Illustration	Work	Reference	Author	Language	Remarks
1.	Acharyatpadam	Subashitam			Sanskrit	

God created us human beings very special. We are born to think, to learn and to innovate. Choosing to remain ignorant goes against the human nature. When does the Learning stop in a human's life? Does it stop after completing college education? We go through various training programs in our corporate life. Does the learning get limited to the training programs we attend? Our forefathers have thought about the answers to all these questions. Look at this beautiful *subhashitam* in Sanskrit given below.

आचार्यात् पादमादत्ते पादं शिष्य स्वमेधया ।
पादं सब्रह्मचारिभ्य: पादं काल क्रमेण च ॥

Ācāryāt pādamādatte pādaṁ śiṣyasvamedhayā
pādaṁ sabrahmacāribhyaḥ pādaṁ kālakrameṇa ca

A Rough Translation in English Goes Like This:

One-fourth from the teacher, one-fourth from own intelligence.

One-fourth from classmates, and one-fourth only with time.

Interpretation – Only 25% of the learning comes from the teacher(s), which can be extended to include trainers/college/company, etc. in modern context. Another 25% will come from one's intelligence, another 25% from peers, which explains why you should be in the company of right-minded peers. The last quotient of 25% gets credited only in due course, i.e., 'lifetime learning based on our experience.' We continue to mature only as long as we learn.

We normally see preference and valuation being given for the number of years of experience. All our CVs loudly trumpet the number of years of experience. Important assignments are given only to those with the required experience. Will a mere number of years of work guarantee maturity? Valuation is not just for the number of years of experience but for the 'knowledge gained from the number of years of experience.' 25% of Knowledge quotient will remain incomplete when we stop learning. 'Learning' must continue until we breathe our last.

> **Best Management Practice** – I always encourage my teams to share their 'Learnings' formally in a larger group. I initiated the practice of 'Knowledge Sharing' sessions with many teams where an employee shares in rotation his/her 'Learning' to a larger group. 'Knowledge' is a unique and beautiful asset. Unlike money which shrinks when shared, 'Knowledge' multiplies when shared with more people. Why is there a hesitation to share?

Realize the power of knowledge, unleash the potential of learning and expand the power of knowledge by sharing with others.

Learning Is Not Necessarily the Same As Education

> "The highest education is that which does not merely give us information but makes our life in harmony with all existence."
>
> – Gurudev Rabindranath Tagore

We have seen that one-quarter of our knowledge is learned from life experience. Where do we get this learning from? We can look for learning from every day, every individual with whom we interact and every interaction. We see many people crediting one of their ex-bosses for everything they learned. We normally look for visionary leaders, CXOs for the Learning. But do we see people who get some learning from their subordinates? I have experienced many 'aha' moments from unexpected quarters. Learning multiples when acquired from all possible interactions.

Where Do We Get Our Learning?

I was once overwhelmed with a stunning response from an 'Office assistant' who replied that he wanted to become a 'System Administrator' to a routine question, "What would you like to become?" He eventually became a System Administrator. I learned the power of 'dreaming' from this. I learned the 'practicality of punctuality' from my driver who manages to come 'on-time' that too 'just on-time' whatever time he is asked to come, even if it is 2.30 a.m. Every individual displays some positive traits to learn from. Every event has some potential to teach us.

The differentiator is 'Do we introspect?' and 'Are we ready to learn from the introspection.'

Is There a Time Limit to Stop Learning?

Gurudev Rabindranath Tagore did not think so.

Rabindranath Tagore is the first non-European to win the Nobel Prize for Literature in 1913. Tagore has covered almost every aspect of fine arts. Tagore wrote novels, essays, short stories, travelogues, dramas, and thousands of songs. Tagore composed 2,230 songs and was a prolific painter.

After achieving so much, he did not think he should 'call it quits' at 60. He worked passionately for his dream project *Shantiniketan* after 60.

"Reach high, for stars lie hidden in you. Dream deep, for every dream precedes the goal."

– Rabindranath Tagore

As if whatever he had done until 60 was not enough, Tagore learnt the art of building a mud house at the ripe age of 64 and built a mud house for him at Shantiniketan called *Shyamali*.

Long before environmental consciousness came into being and years before the world woke up to the benefits of eco-friendly practices in architecture, Rabindranath Tagore, the visionary, in between penning poetry and teaching students at Visva Bharati, came up with the idea of using indigenous materials and local art and craft to build the most creative of edifices in Santiniketan's Uttarayan complex, *Shyamali*.

Figure 19: shyamali@santiniketan

Tagore did not think his age was a limitation for learning a new art and did not slow down the pursuit of his dream, i.e. building a universal learning hub.

In fact, he never stopped his quest for learning. He continued to learn until his last day.

Learnings from Incidents

We include a field called 'learning' in all Critical Reviews, i.e., critical introspection whenever there is an unexpected outcome. We must do a critical review of all the failures to understand the mistakes and learn from the mistakes. How many really manage to implement the learnings? Have you heard of 'critical review of events ending up with success?' I understand that the Indian Space Research Organization (ISRO) has built the habit of doing a critical review of all their launch missions even if it is a successful mission. Review of successful missions can reveal lots of useful information like which parameters went very well, which parameters did not go that well, etc. This helps to improve subsequent missions.

> *"The only real mistake is the one from which we learn nothing."*

Best Management Practice – 'Post Implementation Review' is a very important phase for every project. Proper PIR can reveal lots of useful learnings and these can help to improve subsequent similar projects.

Take Aways

1. Learning is a continuous journey.

2. Look for positive traits in every acquaintance.

3. Learn from all the mistakes.

4. Periodic 'Knowledge Sharing' across the team is an effective 'Best Practice.'

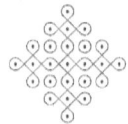

2. Listening Is Gain

Table 7: Literature Reference for `Listening'

Sl.	Illustration	Work	Reference	Author	Language	Remarks
1.	Selvathul Selvam	Thirukkural	Kural 411, Chapter 'Listening'	Thiruvalluvar	Tamil	10 kurals on the power of 'Listening'
2.	AthmaVa	brihadaranyaka-Upanishad	2.4.5	Unauthored	Sanskrit	Sage Yajnavalkya's advice to his wife Maitreyi about the right method of self-realization

செல்வத்துட் செல்வஞ் செவிச்செல்வம் அச்செல்வம்
செல்வத்து ளெல்லாந் தலை. *411*

The above kural exalts the greatness of listening as a skill. Thiruvalluvar quotes that 'listening' as a skill is the greatest of all wealth. Thiruvalluvar reserved one Chapter, Chapter 42, i.e., 10 kurals for listening skill under the name *Kelvi*.

Learning and listening are linked. Learning is not possible without ardent listening.

What are the known constraints for Listening skill?

- Love for one's own voice, i.e., Talking more than Listening.

- Not living in the present.

"When you talk, you are only repeating what you already know. But if you listen, you may learn something new."

— The Dalai Lama

'Not living in the present' is a major distraction for 'listening.' Concentration is required to assimilate and absorb the 'listening.'

Living in the Present

What is the meaning of 'living in the present'? The easiest way to explain 'living in the present' is to explain what is 'not living in the present' since this is the state we have become habitually used to.

When you aren't present, you become a victim of time. Your mind is pulled into the past or the future, or both, resulting in missing the present. When our lives become dictated by thoughts and emotions attached to past events or future outcomes, due focus and attention are not given for the present.

We live in the age of distraction. It is quite common to see people fiddling with their phones or fingering on their laptops during a meeting. Yet one of life's sharpest paradoxes is that the brightest future hinges on your ability to pay attention to the present.

We don't appreciate the present because our 'monkey mind' vaults from thought to thought like monkeys swinging from tree to tree. That is why Indian Vedic scriptures explain the correct process of 'listening' to 'learning.'

Shravanam, Mananaman & Nidhidhyasanam

The process of **Learning** involves basically three steps, viz., **Shravanam** (Shravanam is not just Listening, Shravanam translates to 'listening with attention'), **Mananam** (Continuous Reflection) and **Nidhidhyasanam** (Deeper Contemplation or Meditation) leading to **Saakshatkaaram** (Realizing or Actualizing the Truth).

Let us see each of the three steps.

Shravanam is the first step in learning., listening with rapt attention. Even reading or watching a video or listening to audio can be called Shravanam. The words are to be heard with absolute attention in absolute silence without missing a single pause, gesture, tone, feel or expression. At times, I wonder how great speakers are able to answer all questions during their speeches. The secret is that they do the above process in the correct sequence when a question is asked. They listen without any distraction when a question is asked, reflect and contemplate on the context and purpose of the question and arrive at the answer in between the question and their answer.

Mananam means trying to reflect uninterruptedly on what has been heard; trying to understand not only the superficial meaning but deeper meaning. Mananam should go on for sufficient time until one is satisfied enough that he has not left with anything more to understand.

The ancient practice of learning does not demand blind belief or acceptance of what is taught. The mode of inquiry, analysis, clarifying doubts and assumptions is highly encouraged. This is broadly what is covered in the mananam phase.

Mananam also involves thinking of the pros and cons of what has been said, questioning one's own self to understand all the possible aspects of what has been heard. This should result in a comprehensive understanding of the subject that one has heard.

In this Brihadaraynaka Upanishad (2.4.5) verse, Sage Yajnavalkya advises his wife Maitreyi about the right method of self-realization:

Upanishads are part of Vedanta or the last part of the Vedas (anta in Sanskrit means 'the end' or 'last portion'), the oldest scriptures of Hinduism. It is difficult to ascribe a period to Vedas and Vedantas. The term Upanishad derives from upa – (nearby), ni – (at the proper place) and sad (to sit) and it means 'sitting near a teacher to receive the sacred teachings.' Of the 108 Upanishads that have been preserved, 12 are considered the principal Upanishads. The Upanishads are the record of what the sages and seers perceived in thoughts and visions.

आत्मावाअरेद्रष्टव्य:श्रोतव्योमन्तव्योनिदिध्यासितव्योमैत्रेयि,
आत्मनोवाअरेदर्शनेनश्रवणेनमत्याविज्ञानेनेदंसर्वविदितम्

ātmāvā are dṛṣṭavyaḥ
śrotravyomantavyonidīdhyāsitavyo Maitreyi

ātmanovā are darśanenaśravaṇenamatyāvijñānenedaṃ
sarvaṃ viditam

The Self, my dear Maitreyi, should be realized—should be heard of, reflected on and meditated upon. By the realization of the Self, my dear, through hearing, reflection and meditation, all this is known.

Nidhidhyaasanam means deep thinking based on the outcome of the above two steps. This is contemplating deeply on the essence so that the 'learning' stays part of the system.

Saakshaatkaaram is the final phase of learning where the 'learning' becomes a reality or is actualized in a very real sense, and one is face to face with reality.

Real knowledge is acquired only by following these steps. This is a tested truth, and it has been followed for ages in India since the Vedic times.

Shravanam (Listening with rapt attention) is the foundation for the listening process.

Take Aways

1. Live in the present, enjoy the present.
2. Listen with attention, reflect, contemplate deeply and acquire the knowledge.

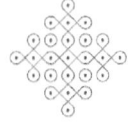

3. Process Orientation

Table 8: Literature Reference on 'Process Orientation'

Sl.	Illustration	Work	Reference	Author	Language	Remarks
1.		Koil Ozhugu		Ramanujar	Tamil	
2.		Arthashastra	Chapter 19, Section 37	Kautilya	Sanskrit	'Standardization of weights and measures'

We have seen Guru Ramanujar's Determination in Section A. Ramanujar was an expert in Process Reengineering as well! Yes, Ramanujar was the first to structure a 'Quality Management System' standard about 1000 years before ISO could frame the ISO 9001 standard!

Srirangam is the spiritual abode of Lord Ranganathar, the incarnation of Lord Vishnu. Srirangam is the first in the list of 108 coveted spiritual destinations for Srivaishnavaites called '108 Thirupathis.' Ramanujar established his headquarters at Srirangam and made it a centre for spiritual learning.

Citizens of Srirangam wanted Ramanujar to streamline the administration of Srirangam Ranganatha Swamy Temple considered as the 'Bhooloka Vaikuntam' meaning 'Lord's abode on Earth.'

Ramanujar completely overhauled the administrative system. He wrote and brought into force a manual called

Koil Ozhugu setting out in detail how the daily poojas and 'utsavams' the temple festivals should be conducted throughout the year and how the supporting services should be organized. Koil Ozhugu literally means the Chronicles of The Temple (Srirangam is referred to as 'Koil' i.e 'The Temple among all Temples' by vaishnavaites) and is an excellent record of the Koil *Samprdhayams* and Customs and procedures of the temples.

Even today, after nearly a thousand years, this is being strictly observed in Sri Ranganatha temple in Srirangam. This Process Manual includes the list of tasks to be performed, the process to be followed and the responsibilities (Job Descriptions) for all the stakeholders. He also ensured to include all sections of the society in the administration (broad-based ownership). He created the office of the '*Senapathi Durandhara*' charged with the specific duty of superintendence of the temple. His favorite disciple Mudaliandan and his descendants held the office with great distinction for almost two centuries. Mudaliandan was the first known Management Representative for the Quality Management System designed by Ramanujacharya 1,000 years ago.

The concept of quality and the pursuit of quality in daily life and work were deeply embedded in Indian Culture right from the ancient days. Arthashastra of Kautilya, created during fourth century BC, dealt in detail every aspect of creation and management of wealth. The classical Indian literature used 'Guna' and 'Dosha' to represent good and poor qualities respectively. Many of the concepts of modern Quality Management System (ISO 9001) are found in Arthshastra. Arthashastra established the posts of 'Superintendent of Measurement' and 'Superintendent of Standardization,' which are the elements of contemporary Quality Management System. Kautilya has documented the 'Job Descriptions' and 'Process Manuals' of various essential posts for a kingdom.

Let us look at some samples of the wisdom from 'Arthasasthra' Chapter 19, Section 37 is 'Standardization of Weights and Measures.' This describes the process of standardization of various measures following in the kingdom. Sample this

- *88 white mustard seeds make one masaka of silver.*

- *16 of these make one dharana or 20 simba-beans.*

- *He (Superintendent of Measurement) should cause a stamping (of the weights and measures) every four months.*

- *Penalty for unstamped (Weights, etc.) is 27 panas and a quarter.*

- *Traders shall pay a stamping fee amounting to one kakani every day to the 'Superintendent of Standardization.'*

Can you believe that Kautilya wrote about the best practices for 'Disaster Management and Business Continuity' in his Arthashastra? Kautilya had given various preventive measures and instructions for the King to deal with all types of disasters occurring at that time.

Kautilya classified the disasters (vyasana in Sanskrit) into two categories namely *Daivam Vyasna* (Natural Disasters) and *Manusam vyasana* (Manmade Disasters).

Kautilya described in detail, disaster management of eight types of Daivam Vyasna prevalent at that time namely Agni (fire), Udaka (flood), Vyadhi (epidemic),

Durbhiksha (famine), Musaka (Rats), Vyala (beasts/wild animals), Sarpa (snakes) Raksamsi (evil spirits).

Similarly, Kautilya described in details two types of *Manusam vyasana* namely war and agitation. Aruthasashtra describes preventive measures as well.

A detailed reading of these shows how 'Disaster Management' is an evolved art rather than a prescribed science.

Take Aways

1. Practice process orientation.

2. Practice Preventive Measures, Corrective Actions and Continuous Improvement.

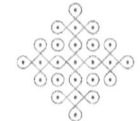

4. Communication Skill

Table 9: Literature Reference on 'Power of Communication'

Sl.	Illustration	Work	Reference	Author	Language	Remarks
1.	Solalvallan-sorvilaan	Thirukkural	647 Chapter 'Communication Skill'	Thiruvalluvar	Tamil	10 kurals, i.e., 1 Chapter for Communication Skill
2.	Solluga-Sollai	Thirukkural	645 Chapter 'Communication Skill'	Thiruvalluvar	Tamil	
3.	Mudivum-Idaiyurum	Thirukkural	676 Chapter 'Modes of Action'	Thiruvalluvar	Tamil	

Communication skill is essential not only for Leaders but also for all job positions. Thiruvalluvar lists three essential skills for a winner and communication skill is on top of the list.

சொலல்வல்லன் சோர்விலன் அஞ்சான் அவனை
இகல்வெல்லல் யார்க்கும் அரிது. *(647)*

Translation: It is difficult to defeat one who is an expert in communication skill, hard work and courage. Good communication skill, hard work and courage with determination are the three essential qualities for a winner.

Though this kural talks about three skills, this kural comes under the Chapter *Solvanmai*, i.e., Power of Speech. Interpretation of this kural extols Communication Skills. Other two are sometimes even interpreted as 'Not getting tired of hard speech' and 'fearless in speech.' So much of importance to communication.

Communication Skill

History has given us many winners who have exemplified these three qualities, hard work and courage with determination, and great oratorical skills. It is a big list starting with Alexander The Great, Abraham Lincoln, Winston Churchill, Mahatma Gandhi, Nelson Mandela and Swami Vivekananda.

Courage is not the state of fearlessness. Nelson Mandela, the South African revolutionary who fought against apartheid and who later became the President of his nation said, "I learned that courage was not the absence of fear, but the triumph over it." The winner should be able to carry out his/her plans in spite of the unfavorable situations and without fearing the possible negative consequences.

Thiruvalluvar did not stop with mentioning communication skill as an essential skill for a winner. He reserved one *Adhikaram*, i.e., 10 kurals under the name *Solvanmai*, i.e., Communication Skills. Let us discuss a good sample from this Adhikaram.

Your communication will be effective if it is clear and uses the **appropriate selection of words**.

சொல்லுக சொல்லைப் பிறிதோர்சொல் அச்சொல்லை
வெல்லுஞ்சொல் இன்மை அறிந்து. *(645)*

Transliteration (Tamil to English):

solluga sollaip piridhoarsol achchollai
vellunjol inmai arindhu

Meaning – Deliver your speech after assuring yourself that what you say is relevant and appropriate. **The words used should be carefully selected so that no other words can effectively replace them.**

Courage and Risk Appetite

Does the quality 'courage' go against the theory of 'risk-based Decision Making'? Courage in business is not to be confused with 'bravery in war.' Courage does not mean taking a course of action unmindful of the 'risk' but taking a course of action without fearing about the acceptance of the action. 'Courageous action' is 'calculated risk-taking.' Good leaders make bold moves. But they strengthen their chances of success through careful deliberation and preparation. Some methods to prepare for 'calculated risk-taking' are taking the key stakeholders into confidence, weighing risks against benefits, selecting an appropriate time for action and developing contingency plans.

Courageous Leaders make decisions and move forward in environments of fear and intense change. Avoid the crutch of 'analysis paralysis' and make the decision. Forward movement is always better than being stuck in place.

Risk Appraisal in Thirukkural

Projects are appraised not just based on the investment and benefits. Modern project appraisals take lots of other factors such as Investment, Time value of money, Qualitative and Quantitative benefits, Risks, etc.

I am astounded to see this kural, which includes Risk as an essential factor for appraisal.

முடிவும் இடையூறும் முற்றியாங்கு எய்தும்
படுபயனும் பார்த்துச் செயல். *(676)*

Transliteration (Tamil to English):

**mudivum idaiyoorum mutriyaangu eydhum
padupayanum paarththu chseyal**

Meaning – An act is to be performed after assessing the effort required (Investment), the obstacles to be encountered (Risk), and the benefits to be gained on completion.

The risk-based approach proposed by Thiruvalluvar.

Hard Work

"You can't cross the sea merely by standing and staring at the water."

– Rabindranath Tagore

> **Take Aways**
>
> 1. Communication Skills associated with fearless execution and hard work can guarantee win.
>
> 2. Assess investment, expected benefits and risks before taking any action.

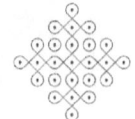

5. Teamwork

Table 10: Literature References on 'Teamwork'

Sl.	Illustration	Work	Reference	Author	Language	Remarks
1.	Samaniva-Aakuthi	Rig Veda	Last Sloka	Unauthored	Sanskrit	
2.	Therindha-Inathodu	Thirukkural	468, Chapter 'Acting after due consideration'	Thiruvalluvar	Tamil	

I could have classified 'Team Work' under the section 'Leadership Qualities.' But Team work is an essential skill for everyone and not just leaders. Every group is to be built into a team, and every team to be made into a cohesive unit. So there is a lot that goes into team building so much so that it a skill rather than a quality. Hence this concept comes here. We often think building a good team is the leader's responsibility. On the contrary, Team Work is the responsibility of every team member. Considering this, I classified Team Work under the Skills section.

Let us look at a sloka from Rig Veda.

समानीवआकूति: समानाहृदयानिव: ।

समानमस्तुवोमनोयथाव: सुसहासति ॥

यथाव: सुसहाअसति ॥

ऋग्वेद

This is the last sloka in the Rigveda.

Meaning – Let your conclusions be alike, Let your hearts be alike, Let your minds think alike. May all these factors make your team an invincible team. This sloka can be called *saṅgaṭhan-sūkta,* i.e., guidelines for building an impressive organization/team.

Let us consider some important points to ponder on Team Work.

1. Teams are essential for any enterprise. A business that does not use teams is the odd one out.

2. It is not a question of how well each individual works; the question is how well they all work together as a team.

3. No individual, however capable he or she may be, can produce desired results without teamwork.

4. You may have the greatest bunch of individual stars in the world, but if they don't play together, you cannot get the desired results.

5. "All the world's a stage, and all the men and women merely players," Shakespeare said. We have to act together for many reasons. There is no such thing as a self-made man. Everyone requires help to achieve their goals.

6. The strength of the team is every individual member of the team. The strength of each member is the team.

7. Getting good players is easy; getting them to play together is the hard part.

8. No one can whistle a symphony. It takes an orchestra to play it.

9. The achievements of an organization are the results of the combined efforts of each individual.

10. The output of a team is greater than the sum results of the individual team member's contribution. There's strong evidence that teams can produce results that far outperform that of individuals working alone. This is explained by the adage, "The Whole is greater than the sum of its parts."

This Thirukkural 462 describes the process for ideal teamwork.

தெரிந்த இனத்தொடு தேர்ந்தெண்ணிச் செய்வார்க்கு
அரும்பொருள் யாதொன்றும் இல். *(462)*

Executing a task with the help of the right people is 'teamwork.' Three steps essential for a good team according to Thiruvalluvar are:

1. Choosing the right people (Forming)

2. Bringing them together (Norming)

3. Discussing before execution (Performing)

Thus, Thiruvalluvar covered three phases of Forming, Storming, Norming and Performing model of group development proposed by *Bruce Tuckman* in 1965.

The following four factors are to be considered to harness the potential of a successful team:

1. Context.

2. The composition of the team with the necessary skill mix.

3. Work Culture. Effective teams need to work together and take collective responsibility for significant tasks. This results in the opportunity for everyone in the team to use different skills and talents.

4. Purpose. Effective teams have a common purpose that provides direction, momentum and commitment. Translating a team's common purpose into specific, measurable and realistic goals makes for a more successful team.

Take Aways

1. Team work is an essential skill for every member of the team and not just the Team Leader.

2. Choose the right team, facilitate bringing the team together and take the team into confidence.

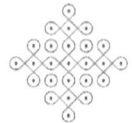

Section C

Five Leadership Qualities

"A truly great boss is hard to find, difficult to part with and impossible to forget.

Don't pick a job. Pick your boss"

– William Raduchel

"A good boss is better than a good company. A good boss would discipline you, train you, develop you."

– Jack Ma

पञ्च नेतृ गुणाः

ஐந்து தலைமைப் பண்புகள்

What Is Leadership?

The generally accepted definition is that leadership is the ability to achieve the right goals by organizing and motivating the team to work to accomplish those goals.

"Leadership is an art rather than science," said Max DePree, Chairman and CEO of Herman Miller, Inc., the furniture maker that was named one of Fortune magazine's ten 'best managed' and 'most innovative' companies.

Concepts of leadership, ideas about leadership, and leadership practices are the subject of much thought, discussion, writing, teaching, and learning.

What are the qualities of a true Leader?

There are many. To start with, Is leadership an inborn quality or is it something that anyone can learn and become a leader? I strongly feel that Leadership is a conscious and consistent practice. Leadership is not occasional streaks of excellence. Let us look at some important characteristics of a true leader. We often hear the jargon 'charismatic leadership.' 'Pomp and Pageantry' are not necessarily essential ingredients for Leadership. Leader's 'charisma' must come from inside. By possessing certain Qualities. What are they?

The concepts discussed earlier in the book, i.e., making your work your passion, continuous Learning, Listening, Positive Thinking, Timely Action, Communication Skills, Determination and Thinking Big are all essential for a leader. But there is more to a leader. There are a few additional traits essential for a Leader to be successful. What are they as found in our literature?

Bhagavad Gita Chapter 12, verses 3 and 4 explain the qualities of the Supreme Lord. Interestingly many of these apply to a good leader also.

येत्वक्षरमनिर्देश्यमव्यक्तंपर्युपासते ।
सर्वत्रगमचिन्त्यञ्चकूटस्थमचलन्ध्रुवम् ॥
सन्नियम्येन्द्रियग्रामंसर्वत्रसमबुद्धय: ।
तेप्राप्नुवन्तिमामेवसर्वभूतहितेरता: ॥

ye tv aksharamanirdeśhyamavyaktaṁparyupasate
sarvatra-gam achintyañchakuta-sthamachalandhruvam
sanniyamyendriya-grāmaṁsarvatrasama-buddhayaḥ
teprāpnuvantimāmevasarva-bhuta-hiteratāḥ

Let us list ten Leadership Qualities as elucidated in these two slokas.

Table 11: List of Leadership Qualities from Lord

Sl. No.	Lord's Quality	Meaning	Equivalent Leadership Quality	Explanation
1.	aksharam	Imperishable	Determination	Leaders don't give up.
2.	avyaktam	Invisible Underlying	Subconscious influence	The perceptions of the leader are internalized and surface externally when needed.
3.	paryupasate	Worship	Respected	Leaders command the respect of all He/She leads.
4.	sarvatra-gam	All-Pervading	Powerful, Sharp	Resourceful, goes to the depth of the details.
5.	achintyam	Inconceivable	Creative	Leaders are creative, think 'out of the box.'
6.	kuta-stham	Unchanging	Concentration Focus	Leaders are focused on the mission and vision.
7.	achalam	Immovable	Steady and determined	Leaders don't get moved by setbacks or failures.

Sl. No.	Lord's Quality	Meaning	Equivalent Leadership Quality	Explanation
8.	sanniyama	Precision, Exactness	Planner	Leaders plan proactively. They don't perform ad-hoc actions.
9.	sama-buddhaya	Even-minded	Even-minded	Leaders do not get carried away by passions, perceptions, mood swings, sentiments and emotions. Leaders take unbiased decisions.
10.	Sarva-bhuta-hite	Interested in the welfare of all beings	Empathetic/ Compassionate	Leaders are people-oriented and take care of the welfare of their employees.

Vision

Having a vision is an essential trait for a leader. Vision is essential not only for every organization, but also for every team and every individual. Every dynamic organization should have a vision. Every empowered team in an organization requires a vision. Every aspiring individual in an empowered team should aspire for a vision.

[1]*"If you can see the invisible, you can achieve the impossible."*

ORAL ROBERTS[1]

How to build a Vision? One has to dream to be a visionary. I already discussed the process of dreaming under the section "Attitudes."

Let us see few other Leadership Traits in this section.

---

[1]Courtesy the book *When you can see the invisible You can do the impossible* by Oral Roberts.

1. Competency Mapping & Delegation

Following Literature References Are Taken for This Trait:

Table 12: Literature Reference on 'Delegation'

Sl.	Illustration	Work	Reference	Author	Language	Remarks
1.	Idhanai-Idhanal	Thirukkural	517, Chapter "Selection & Employment"	Thiruvalluvar	Tamil	

Identifying Competent People

This interesting story *Drona's test for all his sishyas* from the great epic Mahabharata has very often been used in Management lessons, touted as an ideal case study for Goal, Focus, Concentration, etc. The story goes like this. Guru Dronacharya called all his disciples and organized a skill test. He tied a wooden bird on top of a tree with an objective to test who will be able to hit the bird's eye with an arrow. As a qualification examination, Drona asked each one of his disciples to describe what he saw. While every other disciple described different things like the Trees, Branches, Bird, etc., Arjuna was the only one who replied that he saw only an eye of a bird. Drona was impressed with Arjuna's response and asked Arjuna to hit the bird with his arrow, and Arjuna obliged and hit the bird's eye in a single attempt. Thus Arjuna was declared the winner of the competition. Management lesson from this story is generally 'how should one be focused on his/her Goal, blah, blah, blah.' My story does not end here. See a different perspective.

When Drona asked every disciple to describe what he saw, Yudhishtra replied, "I see two trees, lot of branches, green leaves, a wooden bird on top of one of the tree and a distant meadow in between the trees and a young boy leading a struggling old lady to a distant pond. My mind is disturbed by seeing the plight of the old lady, and I should do something about it when I become the King." Drona was impressed with this response too.

Drona rejected Yudhishtra for the archery test but opined that Yudhishtra was destined to become a great King. Drona decided that Yudhishtra does not have the necessary archery skills but is skilled enough to become a great King (CEO material!). 'Identifying the right skills for a job and identifying the right people for the job' is an important skill for a leader.

Figure 20: Drona's Test for Kauravas & Pandavas

This is what we do now as 'profiling' in modern management concept. Different people have their brain wired differently and different jobs need different skillsets.

Every person can be transformed into a 'Top Performer' as long as he/she has the right attitude. If a person with the right attitude is not able to perform, fault lines lie somewhere else, mostly with the leader. I have often seen in my experience a struggling performer transformed into a 'Best Performer' by assigning to a different profile suitable for the person with the right mentoring and guidance.

There is a beautiful kural, which gives the right definition for 'Competency Mapping' as well as 'Delegation' within seven words. This is the most famous kural generally used to espouse the concept of delegation. The first line explains the concept of 'Skill Mapping' and the second line explains the philosophy of 'Delegation.'

இதனை இதனால் இவன்முடிக்கும் என்றாய்ந்து
அதனை அவன்கண் விடல்

(அதிகாரம்: தெரிந்து வினையாடல், குறள் எண்: 517)

Crude translation of the kural will be as follows:

Find out who is best suited for a task (Competency Mapping) and delegate the task to that person. Four essential components of Delegation explained beautifully here:

1. The task

2. Who has the right skills for the task

3. How do we decide on the right person suitable for the task in hand

4. How should the task be delegated?

Vidal in Tamil is a very powerful word, and Thiruvalluvar has beautifully explained the difference between 'assigning a task' and 'delegating a task' using this single word. You need to have complete trust that the person to whom the job is being delegated will complete the task as required and stop micro-managing. Such a lengthy explanation for a single word. That is the power of Thirukkural.

What a great thought of combining 'Skill Mapping' and its natural corollary., Delegation. Kural has many such 'Pearls of Wisdom.'

Fallacies of Delegation

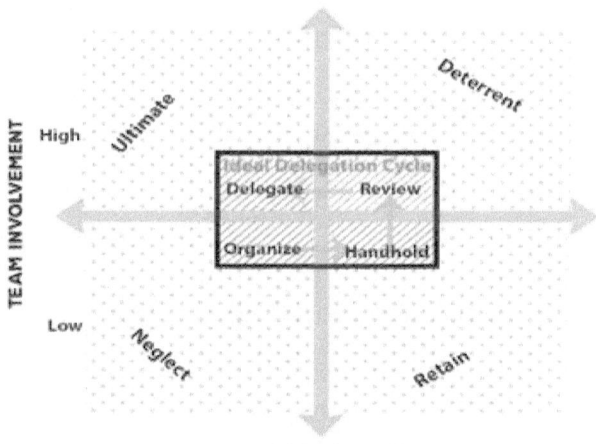

FIGURE 21: Ideal Delegation Cycle

There are three commonly noticed mistakes in Delegation as depicted in the chart above:

1. Those who don't delegate. They tend to do everything themselves. Reasons quoted by them are like 'I don't have any competent person in my team,' 'I get too involved in the work,' etc. They end up taking up everything themselves and end up stressing themselves as well as their team. They don't manage their time properly 'Retain' quadrant in the chart.

2. Those who delegate but don't trust the person to whom the job has been delegated. They end up getting involved in the task more than what is required. This contrasts with what has been suggested by Thiruvalluvar in the above kural. They also don't manage to give quality output as in "Deterrent" quadrant in the chart.

3. Those who don't delegate but 'assign' the jobs, they are not leaders but supervisors who list the jobs and assign the job to available subordinates. They don't communicate to the assignees. They don't give any guidance; they don't empower people as in "Neglect" quadrant in the chart.

A leader is one who knows the right quantum of their involvement in the delegated task. They assess whom to 'delegate' the task. They trust their people that they will deliver the output, but they keep track of the output. They know where they need to get involved and they know the right quantum of involvement. If the 'involvement' becomes more than necessary, it becomes 'interference,' 'Ultimate' quadrant is the ideal delegation, somewhere in the middle of the quadrant.

What if you don't fully trust any of your team members for a task? You still must delegate. Delegation can be in stages.

1. As a first step, you can involve an identified team member(s) with you so that he/she can learn.

2. As the second step, ask the trained team member to take care of the job but take your consent/guidance for all important decisions.

3. As the third step, ask the qualified team member to handle the job but report the progress on a regular basis.

4. As the last step in the delegation, delegate the job to the empowered team member. This is the right definition of delegation as expounded by Thiruvalluvar.

Take Aways

1. Every individual can be transformed to a 'High Performer' as long as the right attitude is there. Transformation is the responsibility of the Leader.

2. Identify the right individual for each task and delegate the task to him/her.

3. Determine right quantum of involvement in a delegated task. This can be in phases.

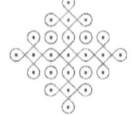

2. Passing the Credit and Taking the Blame

It is quite normal that an average human likes to blow their own trumpet, take credit for things ending up well and blame others when things go wrong. Leaders should be above average. Is this the right attitude for the leaders? Certainly not.

An essential quality for a good leader is 'Passing the credit to the team and taking the blame.' Great leaders do this. I learned this not from management books but from my own experience. I would like to share two incidents from my experience to corroborate this.

Pass the Credit to the Team

In one of my assignments, I was managing a complex technology migration project, which required a lot of hard work and passion. This project used to be the first of its kind for my company and one of very early 'BPO transition initiative from the USA to India.' The success of this project was perceived as very critical for the company.

I used to circulate an email to the Senior Leadership in the company whenever we successfully accomplish a major milestone. A couple of such milestones went by. Strangely, I received a phone call from my boss that email announcements to the Senior Leadership should go from his email ID. He managed to quote convincing justifications to impress his point (Sounds very familiar!). So, I should inform him of the success, and he would then send a nice and appropriately drafted email to the Senior Management. Next milestone also passed through successfully. I faced my first acid test then. I thought about my boss's request/dictum but decided to defy his dictum and chose to circulate the email myself. I felt it is a fundamental work right to take credit for the success of one's sweat. When I look back now, I don't know how I got the courage to defy my boss. I used to be normally known as a timid and subservient employee. It could be the 'yearning for recognition' or the 'courage of conviction.' Either way, I take this incident as a great lesson to hone my leadership skills. To become a successful leader, one needs to practice 'passing the credit' to the team and consciously avoid usurping the credit from the team.

It Is Difficult, but 'Take the Blame'

I had another fascinating experience to learn and perfect the other side of the adage as well. I was put incharge of a cross-functional initiative in one of my jobs. We took a major decision as a team, which later backfired. We thought it was an innovative and path-breaking idea. But our CEO did not like the idea. Of course, he had a solid rationale for his point of view. The point of contention here is not the rationale, and hence I am not sharing the details of the decision. We were in the midst of a team meeting, and I received the call from the CEO. It was the first instance of me listening to the tone of 'displeasure' from the CEO. He asked me in the call as to who took the disputed decision. For a moment, I was tempted to tell him that it was a collective decision. I suppressed the temptation and rather informed him that it was my decision. We later did everything required to undo the damage. The CEO was a great man that he never opened this topic after the incident! The highlight here is that the team guessed everything about the incident by observing the phone call. This incident helped me earn the 'respect' and 'loyalty' of the entire team, which helped me to achieve a lot of positive contributions with the help of this team. I was moved when the team later presented me a memento on their personal expense! I still don't know whether this incident prompted them to present me a memento or if it was a routine act. But, I preserve the memento in my table and cherish this! For me, this will be a constant reminder to the quoted adage.

Abdul Kalam's Example

This is exemplified in the interesting story shared by our beloved former President APJ Abdul Kalam in his own words. Excerpts from his book:

> Abdul Kalam was made the Project Director of India's satellite launch vehicle project SLV3 in 1973. The first attempt to launch SLV3 in 1979, failed miserably. The rocket system plunged into the Bay of Bengal.
>
> Remarkably, Prof. Sathish Dhawan, then Chairman and visionary leader of ISRO, took responsibility for the failure in the press conference organized by him after the failed mission. Prof. Dhawan said in the press conference, "Team worked very hard, but it needed more technological support, I assure you that the team

would definitely succeed in another year." This boosted the morale of the team, and the team made the mission a grand success in one year, i.e., in July 1980. But this time, Prof. Dhawan asked Kalam to conduct the press conference. He took responsibility for the failure but passed the credit for the success to Dr. Kalam. That is why ISRO still fondly remembers the legacy left by leaders like Prof. Sathish Dhawan.

I see many who see Leadership as a position rather than an act. Some people wrongly and conveniently assume that Leadership is limited to assigning tasks and following-up for closure. They are limiting themselves to a Manager rather than a Leader. A Leader leaves behind assets as well as a legacy.

Leaders Acknowledge Every Contribution

I remember the story of the little squirrel that helped Lord Rama to build the bridge to Sri Lanka.

Hanuman found out that Mata Sita was imprisoned by Ravana in Lanka. Rama and his army had to cross the ocean to reach Lanka. His *Vanarasena* decided to construct a bridge across the ocean to Lanka and went about constructing the bridge from a place now known as Sethusamudram near Ramanathapuram in Tamil Nadu.

One day, Rama saw a small brown squirrel going up and down the seashore with little pebbles in his mouth. The little squirrel could carry only little pebbles at a time in his small mouth. He carried the pebbles from the seashore and dropped them into the sea.

Monkeys were carrying large and heavy stones on their back. Monkeys saw the squirrel coming their way and ridiculed the squirrel. But the squirrel did not give up. He said "I'm helping Rama build the bridge. And I want to work hard for him." Monkeys laughed at the squirrel on hearing this.

The squirrel did not think this funny at all. He said, "Look, I can't carry mountains or rocks. God gave me only a little strength. I can only carry pebbles. My heart cries out for Rama, and I'll do all I can for him," and continued to focus on his job. Monkeys got angry and one of them picked up the squirrel by his tail and threw him far away. The squirrel, crying out the name of Rama, fell into his hands.

Rama held the squirrel close to him and said to the monkeys, "Do not make fun of the weak and the small. Your strength or what you do is not important. What matters is the determination to contribute and the love and passion in work. O Vanaras, you are brave and strong and are doing a wonderful job bringing all these huge boulders and stones from far and dropping them in the ocean. But did you notice that it is the tiny pebbles and stones brought by this small squirrel and some of the other smaller creatures which are filling the small gaps left between the huge stones? Further, don't you realize that the tiny grains of sand brought by this squirrel are the ones which bind the whole structure and make it strong?"

Rama continued, "Always remember, however small, every task is equally important. A project can never be completed by the mainline people alone.

They need the support of everyone, and however small, an effort should always be appreciated!"

Rama then turned to the squirrel and said softly, "My dear squirrel, I am sorry for the hurt caused to you by my army and thank you for the help you have rendered to me. Please go and continue your work happily." Saying this, he gently stroked the back of the squirrel with his fingers, and three lines appeared where the Lord's fingers had touched it. It is said that squirrels are born with three lines on their back after this.

Figure 22: Monkeys Building the Bridge to Lanka

Moral of the Story

No task and service, however small, is unimportant! Every task should be looked upon as an essential contribution. In a project, people with different skillsets must work together for the success of the project.

True Leaders Pull the Thumb Before They Point the Finger

Level 5 Leaders do this exactly. Who is a 'Level 5 Leader'?

Level 5 Leadership[1]

Level 5 Leaders are modest, shy and fearless and possess the capability to transform an organization from good to great without portraying themselves. They prefer talking about the company and the contribution of other people but rarely about their role or achievements. They are the nurturing leaders who do not want credit but want success to sustain over a longer period of time, long after they are gone.

Level 5 Leaders stay humble and grounded always.

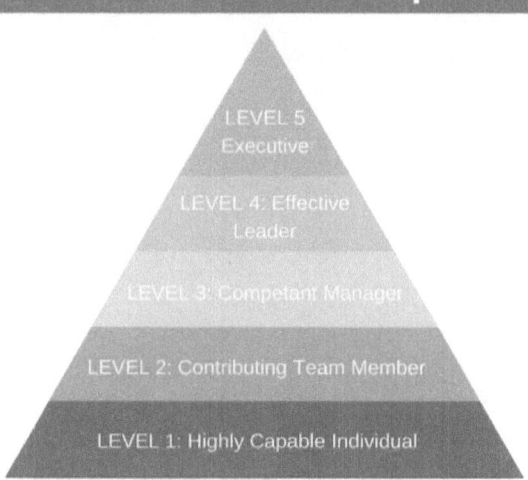

Figure 23: Level 5 Leadership

Windows and Mirror Leadership Model[2]

This is explained as 'Windows and Mirror Leadership Model' by Jim Collins, a simple and powerful concept adapted by Leaders of 'Good to Great' companies.

Take Aways

1. Consistently and consciously practice the art of Passing the Credit for the success to the team and taking the blame for the failures. This may result in temporary losses but long term gains are phenomenal.

2. Stay humble and grounded.

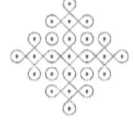

[1 & 2] Adapted from the book *Good to Great* by Jim Collins

[1]Look out the window and give credit to those responsible for positive outcomes.

[2]Look in the mirror and take ownership of negative outcomes. This is even more critical but critical.

3. Lead by Example

"Be the change that you wish to see in the world." – said the greatest leader of the 20th century, Mahatma Gandhi.

He achieved the rare distinction of leading billions of people. He spent most of his life living what he preached to others.

'Leading by Example' is an important characteristic of a true leader. A leader must become the change they want to see in their team or organization. "Actions speak louder than words." Leaders have to take the accountability of 'Walking the Talk.' How can we expect others to change if we aren't ready to change ourselves?

A good leadership role model sets high standards of accountability for themselves and their behaviors. Before motivating the team, a Leader has to remain self-motivated. Be the sort of person others can get behind and support. Be a good role model. When leaders say one thing, but do another, they lose trust—a critical element of exemplary leadership.

Have you experienced a boss who tells everyone to work hard and late but leaves promptly by 5 p.m. to play golf? Have you experienced a boss who talks about the evils of spending too much time on Social Media but spends a lot of time on Social Media himself? These leaders practice the philosophy 'Do as I say, not as I do.' These leaders invariably lose the trust of their people. They create gloom in the organization. They demoralize everyone.

I heard a lot of stories during my childhood days. But this story from the life of 'Ramakrishna Paramahamsa' on 'Leading by Example' made a lasting impact in me. This story always flashes in me whenever I advise anyone. Ramakrishna Paramahamsa was a well-respected spiritual leader from India. He was the mentor and motivator of Swami Vivekananda who stormed the world with his 'Sisters and Brothers of America' speech as a Hindu monk in the Parliament of the World's Religions in Chicago, on 1893.

One day, an old lady came to Ramakrishna Paramahamsa with her ten-year-old grandson. She prostrated before him and said, "Master! I have come to seek your advice for my grandson. My grandson lost his father and mother when he was just a child of five. I have been taking care of him. He is very fond of sweets. He eats so much that his health is deteriorating by the day. The doctors have advised him not to eat sweets, but he does not pay any heed to their advice. However, he has great respect and admiration for you. Please advise him to stop eating sweets."

Ramakrishna said, "Mother, don't worry, come with your grandson after one month." The old woman was disappointed but thanked him and took her leave.

Exactly a month later, she came back with her grandson. Ramakrishna made the boy sit beside him and said, "My dear boy, remember, one's real wealth is health. Unless you take proper care of your health you will not be able to grow into a strong and healthy young man. You will not be able to do anything great in life if you are weak. When something that we eat does not suit our constitution, we should give up eating that item. From tomorrow you should not eat sweets. You are a nice boy and will listen to me, will you not?" The boy nodded his head and promised that he would not eat sweets.

The old woman was angry. She sent the boy on some errand and asked Paramahamsa, "Master, this advice could have been given on our last visit itself. We could have avoided another trip."

Ramakrishna replied with an understanding smile, "Mother, I myself used to eat lots of sweets then. How can I advise the boy to do something that I am not doing myself? One has no right to preach anything to others before practicing it himself. So I asked for some time. This one month I did not eat any sweet. So I have earned the right to advise your grandson." The old woman marveled at the righteous conduct of Ramakrishna. She fell at his feet and took leave.

Figure 24: Ramakrishna Paramahamsa

There's an old saying about the difference between a Manager and a leader, "Managers do things right. Leaders do the right things. "A leader's responsibility is to inspire and motivate people around them. To do that, a leader has to show the way by doing it themselves.

Take Aways

1. If you ask a co-worker to do something, make sure you do it yourself.

2. If you implement new rules for the office, then follow those rules just as closely as you expect everyone else to follow them. If you are not able to follow for a reason, make it a habit of asking sorry for not being able to follow.

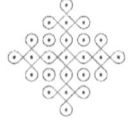

---

[1]I read little different versions of the anecdote about 'Ramakrishna Paramahamsa.' However, the learning is the same in all versions, i.e. 'Practice before you Preach.'

4. Confidence Building

Table 13: Literature References on Confidence Building

Sl.	Illustration	Work	Reference	Author	Language	Remarks
1.	Hanuman Hari Rajasya	Valmiki Ramayanam	Kishkinda - kandam- sargam- 4.66	Valmiki	Sanskrit	38 slokas on Confidence Building.
2.	Dhumena- avriyate	Bhagavad Gita	Chapter 3, Karma Yoga sloka 38	Compiled by Vyasa	Sanskrit	

All of us human beings crave for positive reinforcements. Confidence is vital for all achievements. How to acquire confidence, then? Confidence is a state of mind and not a skill that can be learned. Confidence comes from feelings of well-being, self-esteem and belief. Low confidence can be a result of many factors including fear of the unknown, **criticism**, low self-esteem, feeling unprepared, poor time management, lack of knowledge and previous failures.

Confidence is not a static measure. Confidence to perform roles and tasks can increase or decrease. Confidence changes because of ourselves or because of interaction with people around us. Thus, it is our responsibility to boost the confidence of our people and our teams.

Lack of self-esteem spoils confidence. Confidence and Self-esteem are not one and the same though they are linked. Confidence is 'how we feel about our ability to perform tasks' whereas Self-esteem is 'how we feel about ourselves, whether or not we feel worthy or valued.' People with low self-esteem generally suffer from low confidence, but people with good self-esteem can also have low confidence. Though every individual has to take measures to boost their confidence, leaders have a role in boosting the confidence of their people. Correction for self-esteem has to come from within whereas confidence can be boosted by self or by others.

Confidence-Boosting Techniques from Ramayana

The epics Ramayana and Mahabharata have copious references to 'Confidence Building' in great details. Valmiki spent one entire sargam 4.66 (38 slokas) in *Kishkinda Kandam* on the importance of Confidence Building. Valmiki describes how the wise and elderly Jambavan motivates unassuming Hanuman to cross the ocean to Lanka in search of Sita.

The Story Goes Like This

Lord Rama sent different teams of Vanaras in different directions in search of Sita. A team led by Angad, Son of Vali, went South and this team had the great heroes like Jambavan, Hanuman, etc. When this team reached the southern tip of the sea (Currently Mahendragiri) they learned that Sita is imprisoned in Lanka 100 yojanas across the sea. One of the Vanaras had to cross the ocean to go over to Lanka to meet Sita. Vanaras were filled with fear and anxiety and started discussing the ways to cross the ocean safely. Angad gave a motivational speech to his team as the Leader of the team, "I have heard and known that you all have great prowess and strength. We should fulfill this task of finding Sita, and without that, we cannot return to our land. Confirm to me your willingness to take up this task and describe your strength to achieve this tough task?"

On hearing this, each Vanara confidently gave numbers starting from ten yojanas upto 90 yojanas, 10 yojanas incremental. Angad knew that 90 yojanas were not enough to cross the ocean. Angad could cross the 100 yojanas but not able to return. As a leader 'leading from the front,' he offered himself for the mission as no one else was exhibiting confidence. During this entire discussion, Hanuman was sitting alone, silent, and did not offer any opinion. Jambavan, the master strategist, knew that Hanuman was best suited for the challenge. He took up the responsibility of motivating Hanuman to take up the challenge by boosting his confidence. How Jambavan went about boosting Hanuman's confidence is an interesting lesson for leaders. Let us look at a few important slokas from the 38 slokas of Jambavan's confidence-boosting measures. All the 38 slokas are monologues from Jambavan and they explain various techniques that can be used for Confidence Building.

Figure 25: Jambavan mentoring Hanuman in Ramayana

हनुमन्हरिराजस्यसुग्रीवस्यसमोहिअसि ।
रामलक्ष्मणयो:चअपितेजसाचबलेनच ॥ ४-६६-३

Hanuman, "By your brilliance and brawn, oh you are equal to the King of monkeys, Sugreeva, or even to Rama and Lakshmana, as well."

Thus Jambavan starts by equating Hanuman to Sugreeva, his boss, even to Rama and Lakshmana, who are his role models. This is a powerful technique for Confidence Building. Start with a big impact. Role models and positive quotes can do wonders.

पक्षयो:यत्बलम्तस्यतावत्भुजबलम्तव ।
विक्रम:चअपिवेग:चनतेतेनअपहीयते ॥ ४-६६-६

Your arms are as powerful as the wings of the divine bird Garuda, who is superbly mighty in speed and is also daring.

Then he equates the power of his arms to the power of the divine bird Garuda's wings. Jambavan also mentions in a previous sloka that Garuda regularly crosses oceans and picks reptiles from the oceans. The challenge in hand is crossing the ocean. By equating to Garuda, Jambavan wisely indicates to Hanuman that he is very much capable of crossing the ocean. Jambavan now gives the confidence that Hanuman has the necessary tools and techniques to accomplish the task.

Explain tools, techniques and skills in possession to remove the fear. Explain the real worth and build the trust that the discussion is not hollow jargon.

बलम्बुद्धिःचतेजःचसत्त्वम्चहरिसत्तम ।
विशिष्टम्सर्वभूतेषुकिम्आत्मानम्नसज्जसे ॥ ४-६६-७

You are the finest among all beings by dint of your force, faculty, flair and fortitude. Why then is there hesitation in your task of leaping the ocean?

Here Jambavan says that Hanuman has every quality necessary for the given challenge and also takes a dig at his 'lack of confidence.'

Then in other slokas, Jambavan explains the rationale for his confidence in the strength of Hanuman by reminding him that he is the son of Vayu, the Lord of Wind, and few of his childhood adventures.

Explain the rationale for the confidence especially highlighting previous successes so that the receiving party feels the authenticity of the speaker.

अभ्युत्थितम्ततःसूर्यम्बालोदृष्ट्वामहावने ।
फलंचेतिजिघृक्षुस्त्वमुत्प्लुत्याभ्युत्पतोदिवम् – यद्वा –
फलम्चइतिजिघृक्षुःत्वम्उत्प्लुत्यअभिउत्पतोदिवम् ॥ ४-६६-२१

When you were a boy you saw the just risen sun in the vastness of the forest, and deeming it to be a just ripened reddish fruit, and thinking it to be the best catch, you hopped up and flew towards the sun in the sky.

Here, Jambavan narrates a childhood adventure of Hanuman, making the challenge at hand much easier.

Narrate instances of previous success. Don't talk about failures.

उत्तिष्ठहरिशार्दूललंघयस्वमहाअर्णवम् ।
पराहिसर्वभूतानाम्हनुमन्यागति:तव ॥ ४-६६-३६

"Arise, oh lion-like monkey, leap over this vast ocean, oh Hanuman, your escape velocity is indeed unlike that of all the other beings."

Jambavan concluded his long speech and persuaded Hanuman to get ready for the action. Hanuman increased his size and took a giant leap across the ocean with confidence. The rest is history, rather, of mythological proportions...

Hanuman did wonders at Lanka. But we cannot ignore the role of Jambavan in preparing him for the wonders. Jambavans are also as important as Hanumans in every team.

All successful men would have faced Jambavans on many occasions. We need more Jambavans in our corporate life. Let us ask ourselves, "How many Hanumans can I develop?"

We don't have to wait for a Jambavan. We can do the 'positive reinforcement' to ourselves to boost our confidence.

A Simple Technique to Positively Reinforce Our Mind

Think of five 'positive reinforcement' statements about you such as 'I remain strong and healthy,' 'I am hardworking,' 'I am honest and trustworthy,' 'I will work hard to achieve my dream,' etc. Say all the five reinforcement statements out loud, two times daily. Adding to this, at the end of each day, think of instances where you had the opportunity to prove the five 'positive reinforcements' and where you felt a need for improvement. You will realize the power of this simple technique if we do this every day without fail.

Why Did Hanuman Have to Be Reminded of His Capabilities?

Let us rewind and think why Hanuman had to be reminded of his capabilities. If Hanuman was so powerful and achieved wonders in his childhood, why was it necessary to bring in Jambavan to give the confidence-boosting speech? Why did Hanuman not volunteer his services to cross the ocean? Was it due to 'indifference' or 'lack of seriousness in the mission?' Certainly not. It's not expected from Hanuman who had already accepted 'Rama' as his master. Then why? Hanuman was not aware of his 'flying capabilities.'

The story goes like this. Hanuman is the son of Wind God Vayu. Hanuman got his divine power to fly as a boon from Indra and other Gods. Armed with this power, Hanuman got mischievous as a child. Hanuman would disturb Rishi's tapas by taking away their articles and flying away. Annoyed at this, Rishis cursed Hanuman that he would lose his flying power. His mother, Anjana, pleaded with the Rishis for forgiveness.

Rishis relented and modified the curse that Hanuman will forget his 'flying powers' till reminded about it by a wise man at an appropriate time.

Hanuman Phenomenon

The story might sound absurd for a rationalist. Flying power, curses and boon? Actually, if you look at the inner meaning and the learning it gives, it's not absurd. We would have faced the *'Hanuman Hurdle'* on many occasions in our life. I have seen many Hanumans. I went through the Hanuman Phenomenon many times myself. We get many Hanumans in our teams who do not readily realize their capabilities. They are not aware of their capabilities. They do not readily grab opportunities because they are unsure of themselves. Most of us get afflicted with the 'Hanuman Phenomenon' at times. **Each and every human who has taken birth in this wonderful world has tremendous potential called the 'intellectual power,' which can be harnessed exponentially, but we are not aware of the full potential of our mind.**

Okay. What is this politically incorrect story about 'curse'? Curse in the story is not illogical but 'vital learning.' We face curses in many forms. These curses are constant negative vibes—negative feedback, fear, trauma, moving with negative minded people, constant criticism, etc. Anybody will forget their power (i.e. lose confidence) under the influence of these curses until a mentor like Jambavan arrives. We don't need to wait for a Jambavan to realize our potential. We can transform ourselves. But there are many Hanumans who wait for their Jambavans. Good mentors can create a 'wow effect' even on those who suffer from 'low confidence.'

Being around negative people can drain your energy and cause you to feel trapped and overwhelmed. Learning to recognize the negative people in your life, and finding ways to avoid them, will result in a more sustainable and satisfying life for you.

Avoid negative people for they are the greatest destroyers of self-confidence and self-esteem. Surround yourself with people who bring out the best in you.

Indian mythology is one of the richest in the World. Unlike other cultures, mythology in the Indian context is still a part of our lives, believed and beloved. They are quoted for all day-to-day needs and still have strong inspirational value. Indian Literature explains models and behavior for our daily life. They have tremendous hold and power over our people. They are not only stories of Dharma but of 'positive living.'

Negative Thinking Is Akin to Carrying 20 Bags on the Luggage

Dr. Kalam had positive impacts from many of his mentors. Dr. Brahma Prakash was one of them. Dr. Kalam mentioned that Dr. Brahma Prakash changed the way he saw the world. He once told Kalam, "Kalam, if you see this world as mean and rude, it will interfere with your concentration. Negative thinking is similar to carrying 20 bags of luggage on a trip. This baggage will make your trip miserable, and progress will be slow."

Negative Feelings Hinder Our Potential

I find this quote from Bhagavad Gita, Karma Yoga Chapter 3 as a reinforcement of the belief that negative thinking is a stumbling block for growth.

धूमेनाव्रियतेवह्निर्यथादर्शोमलेनच ।
यथोल्बेनावृतोगर्भस्तथातेनेदमावृतम् ॥ (3.38)

Transliteration of the same is given below

Dhumena avriyatevahnir
yatha darsomalena ca
yatholbenavrto garbhas
tatha tenedamavrtam

Translation

As fire is covered by smoke, as a mirror is covered by dust, or as the womb covers the embryo, similarly, the living entity is covered by different degrees of impurity.

Unleashing the Fire in Us

This simple sloka has a deep meaning. It is like a dissuading curse—everything pure has a covering that can often be misleading. For example, fire is covered with smoke, which prevents us from knowing the power of fire and if a mirror is covered in the sheath, we cannot see what it is reflecting before removing it. Embryo covered by the womb is an analogy illustrating 'helpless situation.' The child in the womb is helpless that it cannot even move. Similarly, 'self-confidence' is subdued by the negative influencers such as doubt, fear, lethargy, the influence of negative minded people, lack of passion for work, lack of vision, etc.

Fire and Mirror in Management Ideals

Krishna gave this simple yet powerful analogy, which can be used to highlight many thoughts. The word 'tena' in the sloka can be interpreted in many ways. Philosophers describe 'tena' as lust or desire. Fire and Mirror are often used to describe management ideals. Fire compares the *veeryam*, unleashed power and mirror for self-introspection. 'Tena' here more aptly describes negative thoughts.

We must recognize these negative influences and must get rid of them for self-realization to unleash the 'firepower.' It is possible that we can introspect and recognize these negative influencers and transform ourselves. This isn't as easy as it looks but it's possible.

"They who have conquered doubt and fear have conquered failure."

– James Allen

Take Aways

1. Be the Jambavan for your team in boosting their confidence by 'positive reinforcements' as and when required.

2. Shun the company of negative people and negative thoughts. They sap your energy.

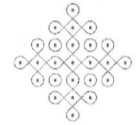

5. Mentoring and Coaching

Table 14: Literature References on 'Mentoring'

Sl.	Illustration	Work	Reference	Author	Language	Remarks
1.	Jyayasichet	Bhagavad Gita	Chapter 3, Karma Yog, slokas 1 & 2	Compiled by Vyasa	Sanskrit	
2.	Karmanye-vadhikarasye	Bhagavad Gita	Chapter 2, SankhyaYog, sloka 47	Compiled by Vyasa	Sanskrit	Very famous sloka to illustrate 'selfless work'
3.	Ititejnanam	Bhagavad Gita	Chapter 18, Moksha SanyasYog, sloka 63	Compiled by Vyasa	Sanskrit	
4.	Nahinaniti	Ramacharita-mansa	Uttarakanda-Sopana 7	Tulsidas	Hindi (Awadh)	

I have read many guidebooks on mentorship. But I find the holy book Bhagavad Gita the ultimate guide for Mentorship. The entire Bhagavad Gita, i.e., 18 chapters, 700 slokas dwell on the dialogue between the great mentor *Lord Krishna* and his devoted mentee *Arjuna*. Let us discuss some essential characteristics for an ideal mentor, and the ideal mentee as well, based on the teachings from Bhagavad Gita. Yes. Mentorship is a two-way relationship. That is why Bhagavad Gita has been conceived as a dialogue between Krishna and Arjuna and not a soliloquy.

Essential Traits for an Ideal Mentor and Mentee

Friendly Relationship – Mentor and Mentee relationship is a long-term relationship of mutual respect. This is something more ascribed than the relationship between a teacher and student. The relationship between Arjuna and Dronacharya was explained at a different dimension in Mahabharata than the relationship between Arjuna and Krishna. A mentor is more than a teacher. That is why, we hear people describing their mentor as 'Friend, Philosopher and Guide.'

Selecting the Mentee – You cannot mentor everyone in the team. Mentorship requires a lot of attention from both the Mentor and Mentee. Mentor has to choose his/her mentee(s). Krishna chose Arjuna to be his ideal mentee among the five Pandava cousins.

Trust – The first and foremost requirement is an uncompromising trust between the mentee and the mentor. Not just the mentor on the mentee but the mentee on the skills of the mentor. Arjuna showed complete trust in Lord Krishna. Arjuna questioned Krishna, argued with Krishna but never wavered on the trust. This is not only during the 18 chapters of interaction but all across Mahabharata. Let us rewind and enjoy the instance of interaction between Arjuna, Duryodhana and Lord Krishna before the start of the Kurukshetra war to exemplify Arjuna's trust in Krishna.

Arjuna and Duryodhana went to meet Lord Krishna to seek his support for their side during the Kurukshetra war. Arjuna got the first choice to select the option between the entire army of Lord Krishna or Lord Himself and that too unarmed. Duryodhana was worried if Arjuna will ask for Krishna's army, but Arjuna was very clear with his choice. He preferred Lord Krishna to his army. Duryodhana was perplexed and thought Arjuna to be a fool and breathed a sigh of relief. Arjuna had the complete trust and confidence in Krishna, and his trust enabled him winning the war. And us getting a treasure called Bhagavad Gita.

Watching and Questioning – Effective mentors allow themselves to be observed and questioned, and good mentees make a point of watching every action of the mentor and questioning them when in doubt. Effective mentors do not browbeat with their point. Mentee must be given the comfort and freedom to question the wisdom of the Mentor. Let us see a verse from Bhagavad Gita.

Arjuna's Confusion

अर्जुन उवाच ।
ज्यायसी चेत्कर्मणस्ते मता बुद्धिर्जनार्दन ।
तत्किं कर्मणि घोरे मां नियोजयसि केशव ॥ 1॥
व्यामिश्रेणेव वाक्येन बुद्धिं मोहयसीव मे ।
तदेकं वद निश्चित्य येन श्रेयोऽहमाप्नुयाम् ॥ 2॥

arjuna uvācha
jyāyasī chetkarmaṇaste matā buddhirjanārdana
tat kiṁkarmaṇi ghore māṁ niyojayasi keśava
vyāmiśhreṇeva vākyena buddhiṁ mohayasīva me
tad ekaṁ vada niśhchityayena śhreyo
'hamāpnuyām

Arjuna said, "O Janardan, if you consider knowledge superior to action, then why do you ask me to wage this terrible war? My intellect is bewildered by your ambiguous advice. Please tell me decisively the one path by which I may attain the highest good."

This verse comes at the starting of Chapter 3. Krishna had given enough comfort to Arjuna in the relationship that he questioned Krishna that his teachings in Chapter 2 seem ambiguous (vyamishrena). Arjuna went on to say that he is getting confused (mohayati). What did Krishna do? Krishna did not get irritated. Krishna took pains to explain and got rid of the confusion.

Perseverance – It took 18 chapters and 700 slokas for Lord Krishna to convince Arjuna. Krishna cajoled and flattered Arjuna as a great warrior and even chided him for refusing to fight but never ill-treated him. A mentor can take the liberty to disagree with the mentee, chide him/her but should never make any negative comment like making a sarcastic remark. Negative feedback if necessary should be given one-on-one and not in front of others.

Altruistic – A mentor should not expect any personal benefit out of the mentor-mentee relationship. The mentor should think of his/her efforts as a noble work for the development of the mentee. There would be incidental benefits like the development of the organization/team but cannot plan mentorship with the 'results in mind.'

A very famous Gita sloka, *karmanye,* enlightens us on this. This is a universal truth that can be applied and used in many situations. Following this advice diligently helps us to remove the stress from all our work.

कर्मण्येवाधिकारस्ते मा फलेषु कदाचन । मा कर्मफलहेतुर्भुर्मा ते
संगोऽस्त्वकर्मणि

Transliteration –

'karmanyevadhikaraste ma phalesukadacana ma
karma-phala-heturbhur ma tesango 'stvakarmani'

**You have the right (only the right) to perform your
prescribed duty, but never claim rights to the results
of your action. Never consider yourself to be the
cause of the results of your activities, and never be
attached to not doing your duty.**

More than a dharmic principle, *karmanyevadhikaras*
is a great management philosophy. Krishna advises us
to do our duties diligently without worrying about the
results. I have noticed in my experience that the concern
about possible negative outcome pulls down efficiency.
Don't we see this in many practical scenarios? Don't we
see 'performance pressure' of higher expectations pulling
down a sportsman from improving his/her game? Don't
we see 'exam pressure' dampening the creativity of our
children? Do your duty to the best of your abilities
without worrying about the results. This gives us the
mental strength to accept any possible outcome. Krishna
immediately counters the possible reaction i.e., "Why
should I do my duty diligently if I don't have the right
over the results?" Do your duties without attachment and
never shy away from not doing your duty. Satisfaction of
completing your responsibilities sincerely is a victory and is
a moment to cherish.

Mentoring is a duty for every leader, and mentors get their pleasure when they realize that they have played an important role in the development of the mentee, and mentors don't seek any other favor.

I am grateful to God that I had the association of a few great mentors, and I got the opportunity to play a positive role in the career of a few people. I fondly remember the special attention given by my first mentor in my very first job, Seshaiahgaru. He taught me the fundamentals of 'computer networking' and how to always stay positive in work. I still remember the special attention given by him—taking me to his house for lunch. If Seshaiah laid the foundation for my technical acumen, Devendra Saharia, Founder and CEO of AGS Health Inc., helped me to hone my 'people skills.' His trust, confidence, enablement and personal rapport are great lessons in mentorship. He is truly the Level 5 Leader.

I have had my share of joy when a few of my current and past team members have expressed that I had made a difference in their lives.

Giving Positive Reinforcement – Humans crave for positive reinforcement. We learn faster and more effectively when we get positive feedback that too from a person whom we respect. Mentors use 'positive feedback' very effectively and generously. Mentees respect mentors. When mentees receive positive feedback from the mentors, they get motivated exponentially. Krishna used positive reinforcement in many instances in Bhagavad Gita. He never undermined the power of Arjuna. He praised Arjuna as the best warrior in many slokas.

Gentle and Not Coercive – Mentors give advice but do not force their opinion on the mentees. Mentors do not expect that mentees act strictly as per their advice. They give the freedom to the mentees to choose their own course of action.

The sloka given below explains this trait beautifully. The real beauty is that this sloka in Bhagavad Gita comes towards the end of the upadesh, i.e., in Chapter 18. Krishna has given complete guidance to Arjuna and had already convinced him. Arjuna had already affirmed that Krishna had cleared his confusion and enlightened him on what to do. Still, in the end, Krishna advised Arjuna to ponder over whatever he said all along and then do as per Arjuna's careful analysis.

इति ते ज्ञानमाख्यातं गुह्याद्गुह्यतरं मया ।
विमृश्यैतदशेषेण यथेच्छसि तथा कुरु ॥ 18.63॥

Transliteration –

iti te jñānamākhyātaṁ guhyādguhyataraṁ mayā
vimṛiśhyaitadaśheṣheṇa yathechchhasi tathā kuru

I have explained to you this knowledge that is more secret than all secrets. Ponder over it deeply, and then do as you wish.

Freedom of Choice as Expressed in Tulsidas's Ramcharitmanas

God gives us the freedom to choose and make our own course of action. Not only in Bhagavad Gita, this concept, i.e., 'freedom of choice for decision,' is nicely portrayed in Tulsidas's *Ramcharitmanas* as well.

"Lord Ram called all the residents of Ayodhya. Everyone, including Guru Vasishth, came to hear him." In the discourse, Lord Ram explained to them the purpose of human life and the way to accomplish it.

In the end, he concluded:

nahinanītinahinkachhuprabhutāī, sunahukarahu jo tumhahisohāī (Sopana 7, Uttarakanda)

"The advice I have given to you is neither incorrect nor coercive. Listen to it carefully, contemplate over it, and then do what you wish."

Mentors give guidance but do not coerce.

Take Aways

- Be a Mentor. Mentoring is a blissful experience.
- Establish complete trust in 'Mentor – Mentee' relationship.
- Be patient as mentoring could be a long and arduous journey.
- Do your duty assiduously without worrying about the results. Irrespective of the result, completing the work as per your satisfaction will give the pleasure.
- Give positive feedback generously and in front of everyone. Give negative feedback sparingly and one-to-one, if unavoidable.
- Don't expect your team to do everything exactly as per your thinking. Give them some freedom to choose their own plan and execution.

Epilogue

These are a few of the nuggets of wisdom I gained from Classical Indian Literature. I have presented them before you with illustrations and quotes. I trust you my friends to use as you deem right.

There is lot more to Listen, Learn, Practice and Benefit...

सर्वे भवन्तु सुखिनः सर्वे सन्तु निरामयाः,
सर्वे भद्राणि पश्यन्तु मा कश्चिद् दुःख भाग्भवेत्।
ॐ शांतिः शांतिः शांतिः

I conclude this book by establishing the positive thought from our literature.

May everyone remain Happy,

May All be Healthy

May All See Auspicious always,

May no one Suffer in any way

Let us program our sub-conscious mind with positive thoughts always.

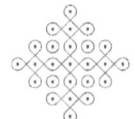

Concepts

'Hanuman Hurdle' – Lack of self confidence because of curses ie negative vibes.

'Jambavan Jolt' – Confidence building to remove the negative beliefs to boost the self confidence.

'Smoky Sheath' – Negative thoughts inhibiting the fire-power.

'Decision Fatigue' – Deteriorating quality of decisions after a prolonged session of decision making.

'WHIM' – Wow! Happy It is Monday.

'Living in the Present' – Complete focus and attention in present not getting pulled into the past or future or both.

'Simha-avalokanam' – Introspecting in order to plan for the next LEAP.

'Divine Leadership' – Leader exhibiting all 10 Leadership qualities as listed in Page 127.

'OHRD Delegation' – Ideal delegation cycle ie Organize, Handhold, Review & Delegate.

'Prudent Optimism' – Feeling of general confidence regarding a situation and/or its outcome coupled with readiness for possible difficulties or failure.